# Walks in Mysterious Northamptonshire

## Marian Pipe
## & Mia Butler

**Published by** Sigma Leisure – an imprint of
Sigma Press, 1 South Oak Lane, Wilmslow, Cheshire SK9 6AR, England.

**British Library Cataloguing in Publication Data**
A CIP record for this book is available from the British Library.

**ISBN:** 1-85058-675-6

**Typesetting and Design by:** Sigma Press, Wilmslow, Cheshire.
**Printed by:** MFP Design and Print

**Cover photograph:** Lime Avenue, Salcey Forest *(Forest Life Picture Library)*
**Photographs:** the authors
**Maps:** Jeremy Semmens
**Drawings:** Sally Davis

**Acknowledgments:** thanks to Colin Eaton for transportation and support and to the many kind people who helped in so many ways.

# Foreword

Like most counties, Northamptonshire abounds with legends and a wealth of folklore. Some stories have a grain of truth in them; others were probably due to the fertile imagination of our ancestors. Whether some of these 'historical' events are true or false, doesn't really matter, because they add to the rich tapestry, colour and 'flavour' of the past.

Although walking has never been 'out of vogue', more and more people are not only realising the pleasure it can bring, but also value the exercise. What better way to get out and about than to walk and be entertained. In this book, the authors have collected together a variety of stories, culled from the length and breadth of this fascinating county. They have woven these – sometimes specifically and sometimes with tongue in cheek – to offer the walker that little bit extra to ensure an enjoyable ramble.

Have you ever wanted to walk in the footsteps of the romantic 16th century Elizabeth Spencer, or wander along the pathways once frequented by a ghostly black dog which terrorised the former villagers of Cottingham? Or maybe you prefer something a little more 'out of this world' as you try to unravel the mysteries of the ghost in Woodford Church.

Or perhaps like me, you prefer to dream that it was right here in Northamptonshire that St Patrick, Ireland's patron saint, spent his boyhood. On the other hand, could it be that you scratch your head and wonder just who moved the stones from the church being built at Church Stowe, to give the Parish its unusual 'Stowe IX Churches' title.

These are just a few of the intriguing, and sometimes bizarre stories which you will find in this book and, when linked to walks, will not only exercise your legs, but in many cases your imagination as well. Happy walking!

*Ron Wilson, Welton*

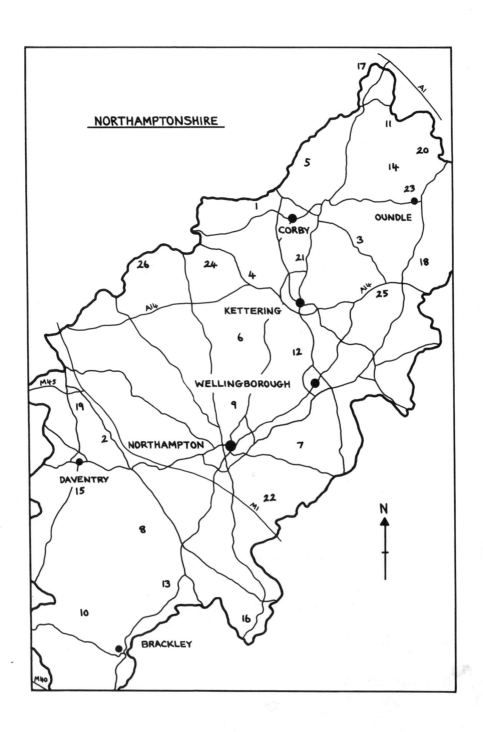

NORTHAMPTONSHIRE

# *Contents*

# Walk 1: East Carlton

*East Carlton Countryside Park – Middleton – Cottingham – East Carlton – Wilbarston – Ashley – East Carlton Countryside Park*

**Distance:** Shorter route – 3 miles. Longer route (via Wilbarston and Ashley) – 6 miles

**Terrain:** Shorter route – moderate. Longer route – strenuous, with some steep climbs.

**Starting Point:** East Carlton Countryside Park GR 832896

**Map:** OS Pathfinders 938 Corby, and 917 Corby North and Uppingham SP89/99

---

**1.** The walk begins at East Carlton Countryside Park, 40 hectares (100 acres) of parkland off the A427, 4 miles west of Corby. The park has all facilities and a very interesting Heritage Centre, based in the former coach-house, with workshops offering traditional crafts to view. On the ground floor there is a well-run cafeteria and a permanent exhibition of the industrial heritage of opencast mining for iron-ore, formerly prevalent in this area.

A giant dragline bucket, which used to work in a nearby quarry, is on display. It is operated by a master crane and large enough to carry a football team. A brightly painted engine, used for pulling the ore-filled waggons, has also been retained. Collectively, these artefacts now form a valuable asset for posterity.

Nature trails may be followed around the park and if one looks carefully, it is possible to find the largest lime tree in the country.

**2.** Leaving the buildings behind, make for the ponds and enjoy the sweeping vista of the glorious Welland valley. Go over the wooden bridge, down through the gate or stile to join the Jurassic Way. This county walk, which starts at Banbury and ends at Stamford, a distance of 88 miles, passes over superb undulating countryside on the ridge of rocks from the Jurassic Age. Note the curious squeeze stile and kissing gate on the rim of the ancient ridge and furrow pastures.

**3.** Emerging at Middleton Hill, there are two fine stone cottages dated 1862, the Red Lion pub and, almost opposite, a stone horse trough inscribed 'I.H.P. 1844' gushing clear spring water. (The inscription refers to the prominent local Palmer family). Take the winding, steep School Hill, on the other side, then turn into Camsdale Walk. Glance over your shoulder at the unfolding panorama but don't miss the old iron pump with an acorn on the handle, a solid reminder of the past.

Pass the Old School House and hidden dwellings nestled cosily among the mass of trees as the path continues along the ridge over-

The church of St Mary Magdalene

looking the adjoining villages. Soon, the spire of St Mary Magdalene, the parish church of Cottingham, shows ahead as the path descends close to the rectory, through an iron kissing gate facing a grassy bank which, in the spring, is a riot of primroses, violets and daffodils.

The church of St Mary has a unique feature on one of its columns of arcades. There are human figures lying head to head; a woman, an abbot and two knights, with visors hiding their faces. This strange group is thought to represent Mary Magdalene, the Abbot of Peterborough and the

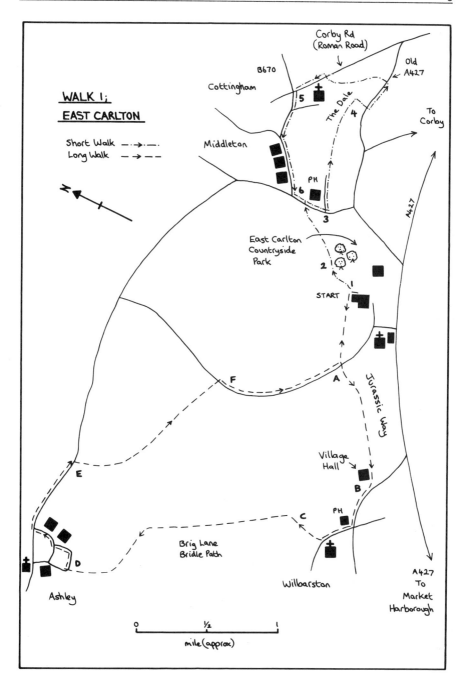

WALK 1;
EAST CARLTON

Short Walk —·—→·—·—.
Long Walk — →— — —

lords of the two villages of Cottingham and Middleton, symbolising the authority of the church, the parish and the two manors.

**4.** After the kissing gate, turn into The Dale, a pocket park where, for centuries, only cows were grazed. Climb the slight slope at the far end to the back road (old A427). In a short distance, a footpath sign indicates left into a meadow, keeping to the left-hand hedge and the next two gates. Follow to the stile leading into the Corby road, a Roman road. Cross downhill, passing Millfield, to the hub of Cottingham.

**5.** Go left at the crossroads (B670) and past The Spread Eagle on the corner, to carry on into High Street. Here you will find the Hunting Lodge Hotel and haunted Bury House. Continue round the bend to proceed along the main street, bordered by attractive houses of differing periods and styles, where the neighbouring communities merge.

**6. If you wish to continue with the longer route, follow the instructions from point A (below).**

**To complete the shorter route**, bear left at the bottom of Middleton Hill and the post to East Carlton to rejoin the Jurassic Way along the entire perimeter of the park. The austere façade of East Carlton Hall is on the rise. This was built in 1870 for the prominent Palmer family, in the grand style of a French chateau. It is now in private hands.

Within sight of the parish church at East Carlton, go over the stile then follow the wall in Church Street to return to the imposing iron gates of the country park. **Short route ends here.**

*Longer route:*

**A.** The second and longest part of this circular walk is rather strenuous, being up hill and down dale. Instead of turning left into the village of East Carlton, cross the road to a footpath between a wooden bungalow and a stone-built house (a typical Northamptonshire dwelling of the 1700s). At the end of the garden fences, pass into open countryside, still on the Jurassic Way. Bear left for a short distance and over a stile, turning right to follow the hedge before veering off towards a hand gate.

Climb the steep slope to the remains of an old, brick barn and stay to the left then continue. Keep the line to the right where a track crosses the path.

In the next field, go left with a hedge to the right. A gap, at a marker, gives access to the track. Descend the steep slope to the hollow. Here a broad track bisects a copse, and eventually leads you to the local playing field and Wilbarston Village Hall. Relax on the bench and gaze at the outstanding view.

**B.** Make for the post pointing to Middleton, on the left side of the sports area, now leaving the Jurassic Way behind. The gate opens to Carlton Road. Turn right onto the path next to the road to Wilbarston. Beyond a small factory, go right at The Fox Inn (on a corner) to carry on to Ashley. The church soon comes into sight beyond decorative stone cottages. The parish church of All Saints in perched on a hill that is bedecked with snowdrops early in the year.

**C.** At the base of the steep hill, on the bridleway, turn into Brig Lane, where a stream runs close by. The path now carries on up the hill. Magnificent vistas reward the walker on looking back over the rolling countryside.

Proceed to a gate beside the water to observe the marker that directs over a series of fields. Ashley now appears, nestled in the hollow.

**D.** At the end of the field turn left into an unpaved lane between high hedges. At the end turn right into a narrow road. Carry on and turn right again to pass Brown Horse Cottage.

**E.** Further on a sign directs to East Carlton Park. Walk across the field diagonally by a row of trees then go through the gap and right on the far side, heading for a wooden bridge and sign. The hamlet of East Carlton and the fine tower of the church is soon revealed ahead. Keep bearing left to a further bridge and finally, double green, iron gates.

**F.** Bear right on the single-track road to East Carlton in front of the church and return through the main gates of the park.

## Folklore of Cottingham

In some of the villages in Northamptonshire there was once a belief in spectral animals that appeared in bizarre shapes or even normal forms. These were known as Shagfolds, Shucks or Padfoots and were often said to resemble a large, black hound or dog. In Cottingham, the memory of such a dog lingers on, particularly among the elders of the community. The late Cyril Loakes, who was born in the locality, was an avid collector of folk tales and anecdotes of Middleton and Cottingham. He recorded much of this information, and one of these tales is of a guardian black dog who appeared on the old Corby road (formerly a Roman road) in Cottingham. This friendly animal would appear alongside the lone traveller at night, as he walked along this stretch of the highway. The dog seemed anx-

ious to protect the traveller, as he appeared out of the darkness and would wag his tail and trot closely by his companion. However, if any human tried to stroke the creature, it would vanish as quickly as it had come! Perhaps there is a remnant of the ancient Northern invaders' folklore in this belief of a guardian black dog. Could this four-legged dog be a Black Shuck or an Old Shuck, the ghostly hound of the Norse God Thor?

## Bury House, Cottingham

Bury House is a Georgian building set amongst tall trees, and is said to have several ghosts which haunt the premises. One of these is connected with a vicious murder that took place in the 1700s, when Meddlicott, the butler, killed one of the maids by pushing her out of an attic window. The ghostly face of the maid has been seen looking down through the glass overlooking the old stable-block, now The Hunting Lodge Hotel. Dressed in black, the apparition of the murdered girl has been observed walking from Bury Close to the Hunting Lodge, once a part of the spacious grounds of Bury House. It is not possible to enter as it is currently a private residence.

# Walk 2: Norton to Dodford

## *Norton – Dodford – Norton*

**Distance:** 6 miles. A shorter route cutting out Dodford would be about 3 miles.

**Terrain: Moderate, but with some steep hills on the gated road between Dodford and Norton.**

**Starting Point:** Weedon Lane, Norton GR 602638. Shorter route GR 594618

**Map:** OS Pathfinders 977 Daventry and Southam SP46/56, and 978 Northampton North and Long Buckby SP66/76

---

**1.** From the quiet Weedon Lane, Norton, follow the finger-post opposite the sheltered accommodation bungalows. Go through a gap in the hedge into a farmyard, keeping to the right of the hedge as the path curves by a dilapidated wooden shed.

Sharp right here as the track goes across the field to a stile and marker. Cross the second field diagonally to the left. Go over the next stile and stay left to head towards a pylon lower down the slope of the hill. Keep close to the right hedge and copse. Past the pylon, look for a gap in the corner with a marker sign on a post.

Go through an iron gate and turn left, proceeding to another gate on the right on a broad track by a small wood. (Borough Hill now lies on the opposite side.) Follow to the left through yet another gate and climb the hill, looking back towards Norton and the gentle, flowing slopes. Turn left, over a stile with a disc, to pass a large pond. Cross the grass to a hard surface, skirting Borough Hill Farm.

**For the shorter route back to Norton**, turn sharp left on the track on the far side of the hedge which lies at the back of the pond, and continue on to the T-junction. Keep ahead on this track to a finger post on the right which says "Byway". Keep straight on to a T-junction and turn left, down into the dip, then up the steep hill to Norton.

**2.** To continue the circuit to Dodford from Borough Hill Farm, keep straight on through the gate and into the lane. Turn left into a field on a wide track, which eventually follows a bridge of blue, railway bricks over the dismantled railway line. The way is stony on the approach to Dodford, which nestles in the hollow surrounded by trees, its brown stone church tower rising on the hill. Follow the path through an iron gate and a row of poplars to a similar gate, with a byway post showing the reverse direction.

**3.** Passing through, turn right, round to a stone dwelling on the corner. Leave the lane to go over the footbridge and stream, where a marker indicates a steep, narrow way to Dodford Church. Through the churchyard, make for the kissing gate at the front of the building. Cross the lane. Directly opposite, a possibly overgrown stretch exits alongside the school, now the Holbourn House Day Nursery.

**4.** Turn left and continue to the signposts in the middle of the road. Go left again and follow the "To Village" sign. Follow the lane up past the telephone box.

**5.** Bear right and turn right by the brook. Keep alongside the water.

**6.** Turn left up a stony track at the byway sign and go under the disused railway bridge.

**7.** Turn left and follow the gated road to Norton, which passes through the farmyard of Dodford Lodge. Your route continues over a high ridge, with excellent views over the surrounding countryside. There are many gates on the hard track, so please ensure that they are properly secured after passing through each one of them.

## Dodford

The pretty, secluded village of Dodford, snuggles comfortably in a hollow on the north side of the Northampton to Daventry road (A45). It used to have one of the strangest main streets in England, as the road was also the bed of a stream for about 100 metres. Consequently, all the traffic had to proceed through the water!

Inside the church of St Mary, which dates back to the Norman era, lies the wooden effigy of Hawise de Keynes, who died in 1329. By her side is the stone figure of her descendant, Wentiliana de Keynes, whose demise was in 1376. She is portrayed on a tomb chest, with her head resting on a pillow, with attendant angels.

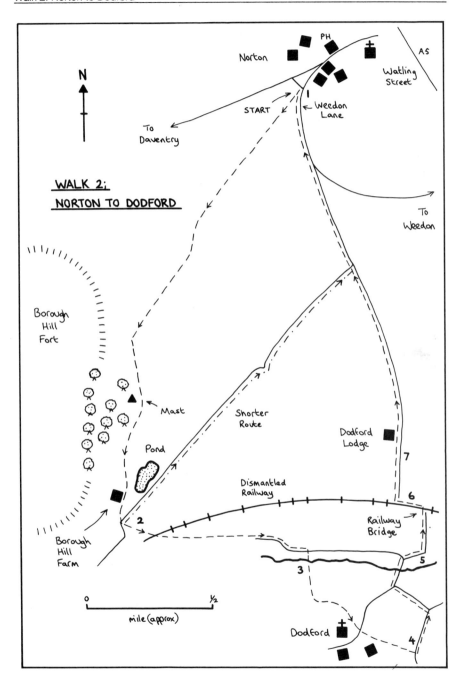

Norton

PH

Watling Street

AS

START

Weedon Lane

To Daventry

N

WALK 2:
NORTON TO DODFORD

To Weedon

Borough Hill Fort

Mast

Shorter Route

Dodford Lodge

7

Pond

Dismantled Railway

6

Railway Bridge

5

2

Borough Hill Farm

3

0   ½

mile (approx)

Dodford

4

Other interesting monuments, stained glass and an arch painting are
within these ancient walls.

## Norton

The neat village of Norton has many stone-built houses and is 2
miles from Daventry. Sir Richard Knightley built the former hall in
the 16th century. His family seat was at Fawsley, a few miles away.
Sir Richard's second wife, Elizabeth Seymour, was the daughter of
the Duke of Somerset, the Lord Protector of England. She died a year
before Elizabeth I and her tomb is in All Saints church at Norton.
Elizabeth's effigy is carved from alabaster. She lies under a canopy,
wearing a pointed head-dress, her small hands clasped in prayer.

There is a charming legend told about the village and its
19th-century squire, Beriah Botfield, who owned Norton Hall. He
had a mistress who paid frequent visits to his mansion, causing folk
to gossip about the scandalous affair. Beriah decided to put a stop to
the wagging tongues and, around 1840, had the whole village pulled
down and moved some distance away from the hall to give himself
and his lady friend more privacy. (The British army blew up the hall
in the 1940s.) The cottages in Tattle Bank Row were said to have
been named after the indignant inhabitants!

## St Patrick

Norton is not far from Whilton Lodge on Watling street (A5) and is
the site of a Roman settlement that extended to both sides of the
main road. The small town was called Bannaventa, where St Patrick
is said to have spent part of his boyhood. His father was a Roman
Christian, Calpornius, married to a British woman. Their son is believed to have been born in Wales in AD398, but the family eventually travelled to Bannaventa. When Patrick was sixteen years old,
the Welsh tribes plundered the settlement and took most of the adult
population into slavery. Patrick was sold to an Irish landowner, who
made him tend his sheep. Amongst the pagan Irish he lived a miserable existence, being half-starved and poorly clad.

He had been baptised into the Christian church and turned to
prayer and meditation for comfort. After six long and tedious years
as a slave, something occurred that was to change his entire life.

Minding the sheep on a mountainside one day, a huge boulder rolled down on him. He was saved by a miracle when the stone split in two and passed on either side of his body. Patrick was convinced that this was a sign from God, and he escaped to the continent, where he became a priest then a bishop.

About 432 he returned to Ireland, where he travelled the country as a missionary, meeting fierce opposition from the hostile Druids and chieftains. Undeterred, he eventually converted a majority of the people to Christianity and founded the cathedral of Armagh during his 30 years in that land.

## Borough Hill

Borough Hill rises to a height of 670ft and is adjacent to the east of Daventry. On the summit there is one of the largest sites of an Iron Age fort and tribal centre in the region. It covers 60 hectares (150 acres) and was advantageous in affording protection to its people and their precious animal flocks, both from marauding tribes and the predatory wolves which overran the country at that time.

Some 500 years later, the Romans constructed a villa on this position, which was excavated in 1852. When England was being torn apart by the Civil War in 1645, Charles I encamped here with his amassed army of 10,000, the night before the fateful Battle of Naseby.

In this century, Borough Hill has once again played an important part in the country's history. The world's largest broadcasting station was installed on the hill for the British Broadcasting Corporation in 1925. A forest of radio masts covered the plateau, as it became the transmitting station for the World Service and of vital importance throughout the fraught period of the Second World War. The BBC ceased operations here in 1992 and the famous landmarks were demolished, although the corporation still occupies a compound on the hill.

Daventry District Council purchased the site from the previous owners three years later, and it has now been made available for public recreation. There are waymarked routes and benches so that the visitor may enjoy the extensive views over the undulating countryside and the benefits of nature in its many guises.

# Walk 3: Lyveden Way

## *Brigstock – Wadenhoe – Brigstock*

**Distance:** 10½ miles

**Terrain:** Strenuous. Although mostly flat, there are some very awkward stiles. Also, it can be very muddy in Lilford Wood and along the green lane near Aldwincle Lodge.

**Starting Point:** Brigstock Country Park GR 955850

**Map:** OS Landranger 141 Kettering and Corby and OS Pathfinders 938 Corby SP88/98, Oundle and Sawtry 939 (TL08/18)

---

**1.** Start at Brigstock Country Park, which some years ago operated as a sandpit. It opened to the public as a leisure facility in 1985, under the auspices of Northamptonshire County Council. Follow the indicated dog walk from the car park to the stile in the hedgerow then turn left into the field.

At the top of Fisher's Hill (a local sledging area), bear diagonally to the right. It is worth looking back to the splendid view over the shallow valley of Harper's Brook and the patchwork cover of woodland and farmland. Brigstock and the tower of the ancient Saxon church may be seen, and further in the distance the slender broach spire of St Peter's at Stanion.

At the gap in the hedge at the corner of Fermyn Wood, strike across the middle of the fields on a broad track, maintaining a straight line to a wide gravel course that separates Lady Wood from Fermyn Wood. Look for a break in the greenery where Lyveden New Bield appears far away, then pass through by the waymark to head for the corner of Lady Wood, which projects into the field.

**2.** Bear left diagonally to the wooden bridge over the ditch, following the edge of the field and keeping the monument on the same side. Look for the finger-post marked Lyveden Way.

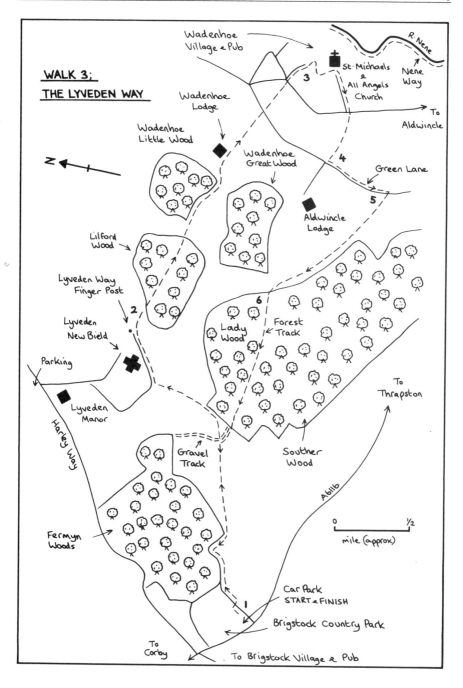

WALK 3;
THE LYVEDEN WAY

A visit to the unique historic lodge is well rewarded, but if this is not on the agenda, turn right at the post toward Lilford Wood, where the trek through the wood may be very muddy in inclement weather. Emerge from cover to pass through the hand gate and head towards the bridge. Proceed over the field, via a further gate, to a hard track.

Turn right, keeping Wadenhoe Little Wood to the left, and go through three more gates to join a pleasant tree-lined footpath. When this ends the way is barred, although the barrier may be by-passed.

Pass Wadenhoe Lodge, a large, attractive, stone house, to follow the farm track to a narrow lane. The spire of St John the Baptist at Thorpe Achurch, rises from the trees on the horizon, and the saddle-back tower of Wadenhoe church is nearby.

Turn right into the lane but go only as far as the finger-post indicating the Lyveden Way. Once over the stile, keep to the right to the far end and the road. Directly opposite, continue forward and down the slope to the gate, heading for the old church crowning the hill.

Adjacent to St Michael's there is a small car park, where a memorial stone records that 'this avenue of hornbeams was planted in 1994 by the villagers of Wadenhoe in affectionate memory of their squire George Ward-Hunt 1911-1993'. At this beauty spot, allow time for a walk around Wadenhoe village, surely one of the prettiest villages in the county and a great favourite with walkers.

From the churchyard, descend the hill or take a rest on the handy seat overlooking the River Nene and the vast water-meadows, or in summer, indulge in a cream tea (Sundays only) at the well-appointed Village Hall.

**3.** To continue the walk, stay in the avenue of young trees from the church gate to the road. Turn left toward Aldwincle for a short step to a public footpath finger-post. Turn right into the field, keeping to the hedge.

**4.** Ignore the approach to Aldwincle Lodge and turn left into the green lane, which is deeply rutted between the high hedges and bordered by the verdant growth of elder bushes, blackthorn and willow. It is extremely difficult in wet conditions, to get down this lane.

**5.** Look for a post about half a mile further on and cross the double stile, staying beside the left hedgerow over the next two fields. At the third, cross to a small copse between the pastures. A broad swathe of grass is fenced on either side. At the next marker, enter the woodland – the footpath is along the outer boundary of the trees.

An inviting wooden bench provides a convenient viewpoint over to Lyveden New Bield, which looms upon the skyline, with Wadenhoe Great Wood to the right, as the leafy path meanders on through mature deciduous trees. At the next finger-post (which directs the reverse route).

**6.** Turn left on to a broad track, dividing Lady Wood and Souther Wood. In springtime, dainty yellow primroses are liberally scattered in clumps for all to enjoy. The track converges with a path from the left at the next marker, but you keep straight on along the stony surface. The path at the perimeter of the woodland bears right and Lyveden New Bield is again prominent in the distance as the walk retraces the terrain to Brigstock Country Park.

## Lyveden New Bield

Lyveden New Bield can be reached from the Brigstock to Oundle road, off Harley Way, two miles from the former and four miles from the latter. There is a limited car park just off the open road, then a half-mile walk up a rough track to the Lyveden New Bield, which is in the care of the National Trust and may be viewed throughout the year.

Thomas Tresham of Rushton was a recusant and suffered imprisonment and fines for his religious beliefs. He constructed several imposing buildings in the county, having vast resources of materials from his estates. Most of these had a practical purpose, but included a mystical interpretation in their intricate design and embellishments.

Sir Thomas built Lyveden New Bield as a lodge for the Manor House, known as the Old Build, which he remodelled, nearer to

Lyveden New Bield

Harley Way. The powerful Treshams depopulated the village of Lyveden, and consequently the massive unfinished edifice remains in splendid isolation to this day. Work on Lyveden New Bield was begun in 1594 and proceeded slowly, until it was halted in 1600 when Sir Thomas was imprisoned. It is uncertain how far the work progressed in those turbulent years. The new building was of local stone and cruciform in shape, measuring about 70sq. ft. It was the only one of Sir Thomas's projects where a professional architect was employed.

Robert Stickells designed the New Bield and the masons were recorded as William Grumbold, whose family hailed from Rothwell and Tyrrel family from Rushden, whose work was particularly fine. The theme for the time was the Passion of Christ, which was closely linked with the Mother of Christ, under her title of Mater Delarosa, Our Lady of Sorrows. The frieze displays seven emblems of the Passion and the incomplete shell carries a plethora of religious carvings. Elaborate gardens surrounded the lodge in its early history. When it was almost completed, at the time of Sir Thomas's death in

1605, it probably had some form of timber roof, but it is now open to the elements.

A few months after Sir Thomas died, Sir Francis, his eldest son, was held prisoner in the Tower of London for his involvement with the Gunpowder Plot of November 5 1605. He was to perish in that gloomy dungeon before being brought to trial. The estate at Rushton was forfeited to the Crown and Lyveden passed to the younger son, Sir Lewis.

After the Civil War, an officer of Cromwell's army, a Major Butler, tried to destroy Lyveden New Build. Having failed in the attempt, he sawed timbers from the walls and carried them off to nearby Oundle, where he used them in a dwelling in West Street, now called Cobthorne.

The New Bield stands in a remote part of the country with the remnants of the water garden. It was intended to be an immense and elaborate garden, with a raised terrace, orchard and fishpond for congers, but was never developed and remained a secret, overgrown wilderness.

More than 150 years ago this was an ideal hideaway for more than one hundred Scottish mutineers. These deserters from the famous Black Watch regiment took refuge in the water gardens at Lyveden New Bield on their way back to Scotland from London in 1743. They travelled by night under cover of thick woodland until they reached the comparative safety of Rockingham Forest. The mutineers set up camp at Lyveden, a haven surrounded by water on three sides and on the fourth, sheltered by Lady Wood, with sufficient supplies for a week.

A message was sent to Major John Creed in Oundle, the closest Justice of the Peace, who agreed to meet them to talk. The next Saturday, Creed rode out to Lady Wood, as requested. The spokesman for the men asked the Major to write to London on their behalf to ask for a free pardon, as they would only surrender under such conditions. At 4am Major Creed returned to Lyveden with a clerk, having already sent word to the nearest dragoon officer that the band had been found. The English cavalrymen had already surrounded the wood, but kept at a discreet distance.

On Whit Monday, one of the Highlanders became ill and died,

and was buried in the woodland. At 7pm the same night, the Justice of the Peace sent a reply to the deserters that a free pardon had been refused and advised them to give themselves up and return to duty. After many hours of debate amongst themselves, the majority of the Highlanders decided to surrender, but thirteen of their number had gone missing.

In June, 107 of the Scots were tried by Court Marshall, found guilty of mutiny and desertion and sentenced to death. However, there was a wave of sympathy for them among the British public and all but three were pardoned, on condition that they were sent to the colonies in America, never to return to Scotland. The three ringleaders were put to death by the firing squad at the Tower of London.

Somewhere in the depths of Lady Wood there is a grassy mound known to the locals as 'the soldier's grave'. A sad legend suggests that as darkness envelopes the wood, the ghostly figure of a Scottish piper is seen sitting on the mound, wearing a long, dark mantle and playing a most mournful dirge!

# Walk 4: Rothwell

## *Rothwell – Thorpe Underwood – Desborough – Rothwell*

**Distance:** 6 miles

**Terrain:** Easy but undulating

**Starting Point:** Memorial cross, Squires Hill, Rothwell GR 816812

**Map:** OS Pathfinders 937 Market Harborough SP68/78, and 917 Corby SP89/99

**1.** Squire's Hill is an offshoot of the A6, which runs right through Rothwell. Start at the memorial cross here.

**2.** Cross the High Street by the zebra crossing then look up for The Crown sign (formerly a pub). Here go under the brick archway to Droue Court, where a massive boulder acknowledges the twinning of the two towns. Cross over Greening Road to Wales Street and continue to Underwood Road. Go right (briefly) to turn beside a wooden fence to Cogan Crescent, then right again into Moorfield Road. Be alert for a finger-post and waymark beside a pair of garage doors next to a bungalow. The waymarks guide you into a short stretch of open fields. (These instructions have simply guided you out of the town.)

**3.** The roar of the traffic on the A14 soon fades as the footpath turns away after the next field towards a gap in the high hedge then on to a diagonal line and stile. Head for a row of poplars that spring from the hollow, then veer left out of the dip and go over a stile close by. Cross diagonally above Hospital Farm and down to the lane in the far corner. The lane leads to Thorpe Underwood.

**4.** The quiet lane passes Cromwell House and Thorpe Underwood House as it descends to the T-junction at Newbottle Bridge. The bridge leads over the diminutive River Ise; follow the road to the right.

**5.** Stay beside the stream for a few metres then leave the road to strike off over the crest of the hill, climbing steadily on the gentle slope of the shallow valley. You will soon be within sight of the outskirts of Desborough and your path filters into Federation Avenue. Follow the steep hill down to the main road, passing the post for the pocket park.

**6.** Use the zebra crossing over the A6 to reach Lower Street. The memorial is facing at the top. Pass the Community Centre and enter the jitty beside the gates of St Giles's Church, where iron railings edge the churchyard. Once over the little bridge, bear round toward the main road again and go up the bank via the kissing gate.

**7.** In a few metres, the first of several such gates leads over half a dozen fields and over the hill to a lane beside the cricket field. Before this track terminates at the edge of Rothwell, pass through the next gate on the left side and go over the playing field to a narrow, closed-in path near the school. This leads to Leys Avenue.

Soon leave School Lane and head straight down and left into Bridge Street (post office, medical centre and shops). Continue to Market Place. Cut through between the pub and the ancient Market House to the lower side of Hospital Hill, facing Jesus Hospital. The parish church of the Holy Trinity has a conspicuous presence in the heart of Rothwell, with a short avenue of trees framing the imposing doorway. Walk through beside the church to complete the circuit at Squires Hill, passing the Manor House, Manor Park, toilets and the old fishponds.

## Desborough

In more recent times, Desborough has perhaps been best known for the discovery of the fabulous Desborough Mirror, the archaeological treasure whose illustration is featured on many an article of local history. Dating from the first century, this piece of intricate Celtic design in brass is now in the care of the British Museum.

Another fascinating item of distinctive jewellery was found near to St Giles's Church in 1876. This is a necklace of gold beads hung with a jewelled cross, which has been identified as 7th-century An-

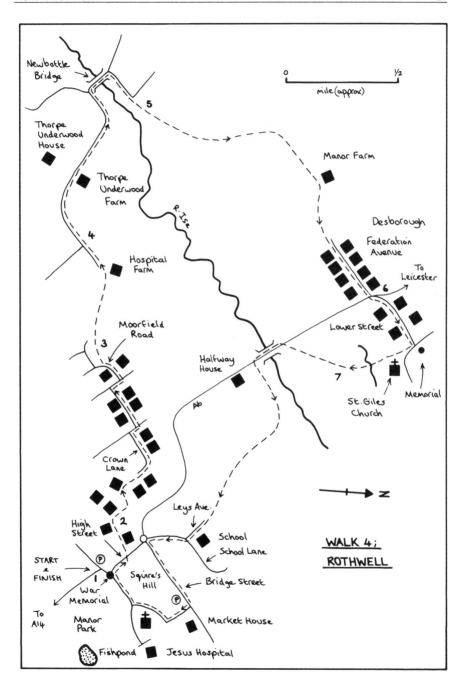

glo-Saxon. Some of the masonry that remains in the church and earthworks to the south also suggest occupation of that period.

## Rothwell

Rothwell has many historic claims to fame but possibly the prime edifices are the parish church and the surviving Tresham buildings. The church of the Holy Trinity, the longest in the county at 173ft (55 metres), has its spire set on a buttress on the north side of the tower. This came about after it was struck by lightning, and consequently toppled, in a storm of 1660.

The interior is widely acclaimed for its remarkable acoustics and for the Bone Crypt or Charnel House, discovered in 1700 by a sexton digging a grave beneath the south aisle. More than a thousand skulls and thighbones (crossbones) were revealed. Many theories have been advanced as to the reason for this macabre collection, though none confirmed. The crypt is open to the public only at certain times on Sundays in summer.

A legacy of ancient, illustrious buildings is to be savoured in and around the centre of the town. In the Market Place, behind the church, is a prime example, which was built by Sir Thomas Tresham around 1577/78. The Market House by 'Thomas the Builder' has a frieze of heraldic shields and the trefoil, the Tresham family emblem.

Knighted by Elizabeth I, Tresham was Lord of the Manor, but was persecuted and imprisoned for his religious beliefs. The vast estate surrounding his home at Rushton Hall enabled him to indulge his passion for construction by giving him access to the necessary raw material – such as stone from the quarries and timber.

In the lower corner of Market Hill, through a fine archway, is Jesus Hospital, now a converted residence for the elderly. Founded by Owen Ragsdale, a prominent figure, schoolmaster and Fellow of Magdalene College, in 1591, it housed 26 old men, who wore distinctive blue coats and relied on the charity of the townspeople.

Another major work by Sir Thomas is Triangular Lodge. This is 2 miles away across the fields and tucked against the boundary wall of the grounds of the hall, yet it is visible from the Desborough road. In this unique edifice symbolising the Trinity Tresham boldly expressed his religious fervour. Begun in 1594 and completed three years later, (dates on the façade differ), every aspect is set in triplicate, presenting an unusual mystery to unravel. Administered by English Heritage, the grounds are open in summer only, but it rises beyond the wall and is clearly visible from the road.

Rothwell, or Rowell as it is locally known, has an annual Trinity Monday Fair, after a Charter awarded by King James I in 1604. The Bailiff for the Lord of the Manor, escorted by halberdiers and a band, parade through the town, visiting public houses and accepting a tot of rum at each stop! No longer exclusively a horse fair, as of old, it has now evolved to become a pleasure fair with rides and stalls in the modern idiom dotted along the main street.

## Haunted Newbottle Lodge

There used to be a haunted house up a dirt track close to Newbottle Bridge, not far from Desborough. Newbottle Lodge has long since been demolished, though this tale is still told. In the early part of this century, a farm labourer, his wife and three children moved into the isolated lodge. It was the only accommodation they could find and had already been empty for some time, probably because it had the reputation of being haunted.

The wife, who was nervous at the best of times, hated the place and kept her youngest boy at home for company. She battled to keep the vast rooms clean, although most were closed-off, and they lived in only a small part of the rambling house. It was a primitive home for there was no running water, gas or electricity, and only a pump in the yard for water. All the children slept in one bed at night, as they were too scared to be separated. Although they knew that no one ever went up there, heavy footsteps were heard overhead and they could often hear bumps and bangs and a dragging, shuffling noise. It sounded as if someone was moving furniture about, but all the rooms were empty. The flame in the lamp beside the children's bed would suddenly flare up a foot high, yet there were no draughts!

The mother's sister came to stay, but the family chose not to tell her about the resident ghost in case it scared her away. After the first night in the house, she rose the next morning white and shaking, determined not to spend another night there. The poor woman told her relations of the terrifying experience that she had suffered in the darkness. Shortly after midnight she thought someone had come into her room for the door had opened and she heard heavy footsteps around her bed. Thinking it was one of the children having a nightmare, she sat up in bed and called out to them. There was nobody there, but she had an overwhelming feeling of a presence, and a menacing one at that. The petrified woman dived beneath the bedclothes, quaking with fear, until early light. The eerie footsteps had encircled her bed for endless hours and her muffled cries for help went unheeded. She had not dared to get out of bed in case she collided with the unknown visitor.

The final straw came one evening as the children were going up to bed, when they cried out that they were being followed. Their father rushed out of the room to fetch his shotgun, and raced to the bottom of the stairs, where he could quite clearly hear the thud of big boots on the treads. Pointing his shotgun upwards, he shouted, 'Whoever you are, come down at once, or I'll shoot you, you b——r!'

There was no answer, but a mighty cold draught swept past him and he thought he saw a shadowy figure hover outside. The agitated labourer felt the hairs on his head stand on end as he fired his weapon into the corner of the yard. Things seemed to quieten down after that and the footsteps were not heard again, but as soon as they could find other accommodation the family moved out. The father used to drink at the village pub a couple of miles away and would bravely boast that he had shot a ghost. He got many a free pint of beer on the strength of that scary tale!

# Walk 5: Gretton to Kirby Hall

*Gretton village green – Southfield Road – Kirby Hall*

**Distance:** 2½ miles, linear. *Be prepared to walk back unless you have a car at each end!*

**Terrain:** Easy, but some awkward stiles.

**Starting Point:** The village green, Gretton GR 899945

**Map:** OS Pathfinder 917 Corby North and Uppingham 89/99

Gretton crowns the ridge above the panorama of the lush Welland Valley. It is only 3 miles to the north of Corby, on a minor road to Rockingham, off the A6003. Not so many years ago, ironstone quarries marred and scarred the landscape between village and town, but it has now been restored to its former rural tranquillity. Depart from the tiny sloping village green, complete with war memorial and traditional, restored stocks and whipping post. The last person to be shackled here, in 1858, was a local man who had refused to pay a fine for drunkenness. He was restrained for six hours before being released!

**1.** From the green by the parish church, turn into Caistor Road and go past a modest cottage, which long ago belonged to a shepherd named Castor. It is known as Caister's Cottage, and left into Kirby Road.

**2.** Then right into Southfield Road. Continue until it peters out to become a lane, which was the original route linking the community with Kirby Hall. Follow the rough track, unsuited to all traffic apart from farm vehicles. Keep straight on, ignoring the branch leading to the Gretton to Corby road.

Beyond the abandoned Kirby Hall Farm, a few fields away, the vista opens to pocket-handkerchief pastures and woodland. Disregard

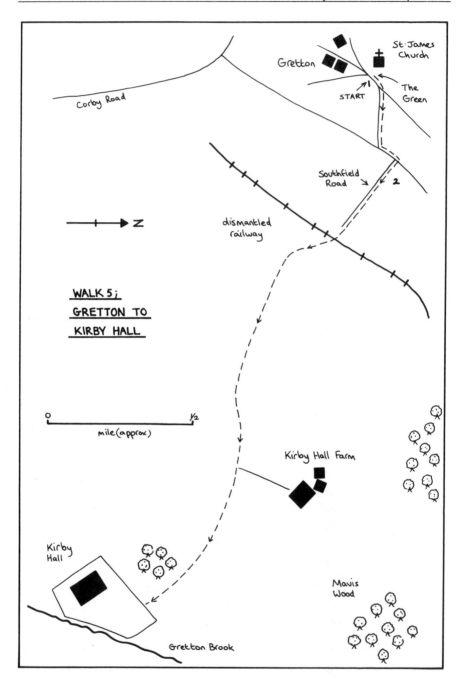

the farm road, to continue the line ahead. At the end of the footpath, pass through a double gate, making absolutely sure to secure it. The field slopes steeply downhill and affords an enticing glimpse of the angular chimneys of Kirby Hall. It also reveals the rich tapestry of the landscape towards the hamlet of Deene. At the bottom of the hill there is a stile in the right-hand corner and a separating ditch.

Over the next double stile bear right, heading for a plantation. The industrial units at Corby become more obvious. After the next stiles, a gate abuts the spacious grounds of the magnificent Kirby Hall. This is set in the hollow and enhanced by the veil of mature trees. It would be a great pity not to visit this mansion of the English Renaissance, which came within a whisker of total ruin through neglect and decay.

## Kirby Hall

Kirby Hall is administered by English Heritage and is open most days of the year. Its striking façade and arched gateways present an impressive welcome to the traveller.

The proud mansion was begun in 1570, at the behest of Sir Humphrey Stafford of Blatherwycke, who was to die five years later. Sir Christopher Hatton, whose principal house was at Holdenby, purchased the estate. He was a personal favourite of Elizabeth I and was to become Lord Chancellor in 1587. It was constructed in the Classical style. With building stone, slate and timber readily available on vast estates, such grand houses sprang up in every county. In this case, as in many others, the existing village was demolished, so as to give credence to the show of the wealthy landowner. The gardens have been recently reconstructed to a plan of 1685, and as a consequence the entire façade conjures up a powerful image of 17th-century elegance.

## Kirby Hall Folklore

When Sir Christopher Hatton, known as the Dancing Chancellor, bought Kirby Hall from Sir Humphrey Stafford, he hoped that Queen Elizabeth I would come to stay. Although there is no evidence that she actually did so, local tradition says otherwise.

In 1589 Sir Christopher held a special banquet in the great hall, after which he led his sovereign down the steps to the smooth lawns, where he bade her a fond farewell. Legend has it that on moonlit nights flickering candles may be seen in the windows of the hall, whilst strains of Elizabethan music are heard as ghostly figures perform a stately dance. Sir Christopher died in 1591, and his nephew, Sir William Newport, who took the name of Hatton, inherited the property. Kirby Hall next passed to the second Sir Christopher Hatton, a cousin of the Chancellor and remained in his hands until 1764. As there were no immediate heirs, it was passed down to the Earls of Winchelsea.

Early in his life Kit Hatton, as he was nicknamed, was warned by a wise woman of Rockingham that at some time in the future his life would be in danger from a bolt of lightning. Sir Christopher was created Viscount Hatton of Gretton by Charles II in 1683. He also appointed him Governor of Guernsey, as a reward for his services to the Royal cause. The Governor's residence was Cornet Castle, a stronghold situated on an inaccessible rock in the harbour of St Peter Port, the main town on the island.

The calamity of which he had been warned occurred at midnight on Sunday, 29th December 1672. The Governor and his young ensign walked outside to take a look at the heavy weather, which was fast becoming dangerously stormy. A heavy scud was driving the sea from the south-west, and the waves thundered against the mass of rocks. Hatton retired to his private apartment in the house he had built two years previously within the castle walls. Kit's house was uncomfortably close to the magazine where 250 barrels of gunpowder were stored. He had not been in bed long before the storm intensified and a terrific flash of lightning struck and ignited the powder, which promptly exploded, wrecking the place.

Lord Hatton, in his bed, was flung onto the walls, which were severely pounded by the raging seas. Amazingly, he was unhurt, but his house was razed to the ground. His tall black servant, James Chapple, rescued his master from his perilous position on the rim of the parapet. Kit's wife and maid were instantly crushed and killed by a collapsing wall in the nursery. In the arms of her dead nurse, his second daughter was unharmed. In the same room, her sister, the three-year-old Anne Hatton, was pinned under a beam, but still alive. Close by, and asleep in her cradle, was the baby daughter of the family. The Dowager Lady Hatton, the Govenor's mother, was killed by the ceiling falling on her bed, but her two daughters survived, although separated by a beam which had fallen between them in bed.

James Chapple had rescued most of the people involved in the tragedy and was rewarded by Lord Hatton with a pension of £20 a year, a substantial sum of money in those days. James took over the inn in Gretton, The Hatton Arms. This cosy pub is thought to be one of the oldest in the county and dates from the 15th century. The fourth Sir Christopher Hatton installed James as landlord after James retired from his position as a servant. He regaled his customers with stories of his adventures on the isle of Guernsey. He lived on for fifty years after the event and was buried in Gretton churchyard when he died in 1730.

# Walk 6: Old

## *Old – Faxton – Scaldwell – Old*

**Distance:** 7 miles

**Terrain:** There are several protracted hills on this circuit.

**Starting Point:** The White Horse, Old GR 786731

**Map:** OS Pathfinder 957 West Haddon and Brixworth SP67/77

---

**1.** Start in the centre of Old, in front of The White Horse. Face the lime tree and seat and look forward along the Broughton road. Take the lower fork, Faxton End, bearing left just before a house fronted by six staddle-stones (formerly used as a support base for a harvest stack or rick).

Pass through the gate into the playing field and make for the slide and swings on the far side. Go down the bank to a stile with an extended tread then slightly right to follow waymarks to cross a plank over the ditch.

**2.** The path goes towards a distant plantation crowning the hill and over the sturdy bridge on the loop of the brook, rising to cross a farm track. A disc shows the way beside the thick hedge and trees to reveal the solitary altar stone of the church of St Denys, the only reminder of the lost hamlet of Faxton. Branch off in front of the house among the trees and go past the barrier, keeping to the same line on the byway. There is now no sign of the site, which is officially designated a 'deserted village'.

**3.** It is possible to take a shorter route back to Scaldwell as indicated on the map.

Shortwood House, situated on the opposite hill and above the medieval fishponds, has a former hawking tower of three storeys that was built around 1720.

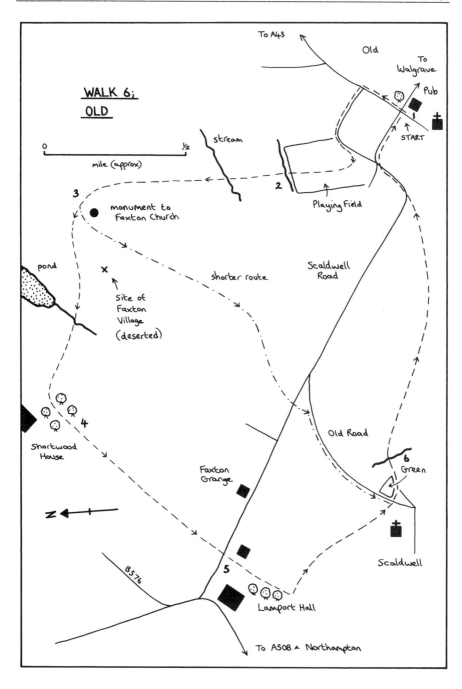

WALK 6;
OLD

To A43

Old

To Walgrave

Pub

START

0 ——————————————— ½

mile (approx)

stream

3

2

Playing Field

monument to
Faxton Church

pond

Scaldwell
Road

shorter route

x
Site of
Faxton
Village
(deserted)

4

Shortwood
House

Old Road

6

Green

Faxton
Grange

z ←—

Scaldwell

BS76

5

Lamport Hall

To A508 & Northampton

Stay on the track almost to the crest of the slope then turn through a small hand gate and on to a narrow path between young trees. Remain on the ridge, with panoramic views to one side of Old, and on the other of the breadth of the valley toward Draughton and Cottesbrooke.

**4.** Exit to the Lamport road and cross to a recessed gateway and finger-post. You are initially in parkland, where Lamport Hall may be glimpsed through mature trees. The walk to Scaldwell is well defined by waymarks, and the Northants County Council Amenity Planting Scheme has placed young saplings at intervals in the hedgerow.

The church of St Peter and St Paul is prominent on the high bank close to the spacious green in Scaldwell. A plaque on the surviving dark brick wall of the early well 'celebrates 900 years of Norman Heritage'. This is on the old water pump, where water was pumped up from the vanished pond to fill the cattle troughs.

**5.** Below the red phone box, turn down to School Lane. This leads to a pretty little dell, a squeeze-stile and a bridge then up through a farmyard. (Please note that this section of the walk is almost entirely given over to pasture, mainly surrounded by cattle fencing, so do observe the country code where there may be animals grazing.)

On top of the plateau, approaching Old, skirt the earthworks before stepping down to join the Lamport road to return to the start.

### Faxton

The deserted village of Faxton lies on high, rolling countryside above Old, Lamport and Scaldwell. It vanished, almost without trace, in the middle of this century.

In the 1921 census there were only 37 people living in Faxton, compared with 108 in the 1841 census. There was no school in the 1920s, nor pub, running water, gas or electricity. There were no metalled roads connecting it to the outside world, only a few tracks and field footpaths. All it had was a farmhouse, six or seven cottages, a number of essential wells, a large village green with clumps of elms, the remains of four almshouses and a simple church which stood at the south-west corner of the green.

In the 17th century there was a large manor house, which is believed to have been built in 1606. At that time, Sir Augustine Nichols was Lord of the Manor of Faxton. He was an eminent Assizes Judge and died whilst on circuit in Kendal, Westmorland. He was quoted by others 'never to travel on a Sunday'. Nichols died without issue in 1616, when the manor passed to his nephew, Francis. A monument was placed in the church to Judge Nichols, stating that he had a 'Christian and comfortable departure'. This disagrees with another source of information which says that he died of poisoning on the eve of a trial of a man accused of sheep-stealing, a heinous crime of that period, The most likely outcome being that the Judge would have sentenced the man to death. The poison was administered by the thief's sweetheart and three of her relatives, in the belief that this action would save the miscreant. The memorial to Judge Nichols was eventually removed to the Victoria and Albert museum in London.

The Ishams of Lamport, who bought the Faxton estate, had the manor house demolished in the 18th century. The same fate awaited the church, which was to be razed to the ground in 1958. Services had been discontinued after the outbreak of the Second World War. The ancient church of St Denys dated back to the 12th century and had an unusual double bell tower. One of the authors (Mia) recalls that she was personally involved with the demolition of the building, and actually drove a vehicle on site throughout her family's contract.

Only the outer walls were left standing, where cattle wandered freely in and out, often rubbing themselves against the crumbling stone walls, thus accelerating the decline of this isolated edifice. As this was consecrated ground, ecclesiastical dignitaries from the diocese of Peterborough had to attend to deconsecrate the holy place, to allow for the removal of artefacts and gravestones before the demolition process.

Only a section of one of the pillars remains, with an inscription that records, 'On this site once stood the altar of St Denys.' Only a rusting wire fence protects this reminder, sadly neglected in a field on the hilltop. When the author visited the site some years ago to look for the stone, she was disorientated by a new plantation and a vast mass of tall sunflowers in full bloom. Eventually, the stone was located, submerged in a sea of brilliant yellow flower heads!

Gradually, the few folk that remained after the war drifted away, and the severe winter of 1947 convinced the majority that it might be better to be closer to modern roads and facilities. The last person to linger there was Mrs May Bamford, who lived alone in Faxton for some time until she, too, left in the 1960s. Hence, a once small but thriving community faded into oblivion.

## Scaldwell

The name, from the Saxon derivation 'sceald' and 'weillel' means 'shallow spring', and there were numerous wells in the village, including a chalybeate (healing) well.

Scaldwell is in a pretty setting and its centre is a handsome green bordered by mature trees. The church of St Peter and St Paul has a Norman tower and occupies a prominent position on a hillside close by. Prior to the Battle of Naseby, when locals feared the Roundheads pillaging their treasures, the stained glass was removed from the windows and buried 'near to a tree'. It has never been recovered!

Inside there is a heavy, elaborate font cover that was carved locally and is raised and lowered by a pulley. There are also embroidered hassocks and Victorian patterned tiles. Just beside the porch are the remains of a stone preaching cross.

The oldest water source in the village was the Town Well, which once stood on the green. The stones from the 17th-century well have been embedded into the wall of blue brick, which is a remnant of the outer wall of the pump housing. The pump previously fed a series of horse troughs from the nearby pond, but this has long since disappeared.

A previous vicar, the Reverend Kersley Kershaw who died in 1930, kept a detailed account of village life in his diary of the 19th-century. He wrote that around 1820 there was a forge on the green. The blacksmith, Thomas Corby, owned the forge. Beside the house and barn below the smithy, horses were watered at the pond.

A village simpleton, Gulliver, was confined to the barn. He was apt to grow violent at times and his food had to be pushed under the door by his carers. This group of buildings was demolished in 1833.

The ghost of Madeline Smith, known as the 'Grey Lady', is seen occasionally as she wanders the lanes and fields, but is never seen indoors. This girl was put on trial at Edinburgh, charged with the murder of her lover, Pierre L'Agelier, on 22nd March 1868. The trial lasted for several days and Madeline was found not guilty on one count. On a second count the verdict was not proven under Scottish Law, so the prisoner was released. She had been under great strain during the trial and when she became ill, was sent to a relative, The Reverend A.G. Douglas, Rector of Scaldwell, for rest and quiet.

Madeline was an extremely reserved person (which was hardly surprising in her tragic circumstances) and had a graceful deportment. Her presence caused endless curiosity among the villagers, who referred to her as 'the veiled lady'. When she is sighted, her wispy apparition is always shrouded in a gauzy veil.

George Clark, antiquary and artist, noted for his fine pictures of important houses, lived here and the author H.E. Bates was a frequent visitor. He is thought to have based his novel *Love for Lydia* on the village.

---

# Walk 7: Whiston

---

## *Whiston – Castle Ashby – Chadstone – Cogenhoe – Whiston*

**Distance:** 7 miles, but may easily be split into two attractive walks

**Terrain:** Varies from riverside path to hilltops

**Starting Point:** The Green, Whiston GR 852605

**Map:** OS Landranger 152

---

**1.** Whiston is about a quarter of a mile above the Grendon to Cogenhoe road, and about 3 miles south of the A45, turning off at the sign for Cogenhoe. On approach to the tiny, triangular green at Whiston, go left to follow the lane around to a facing stone barn and park with consideration in this delightfully English village.

The gate beside the high wall leads quite steeply (though rewardingly) up a gravelled field path on Combe Hill to the striking church of St Mary the Virgin, built around 1534.

(**To avoid this climb** (and omit the church), keep to the lane and continue up the hill on the country road. Here you will shortly be joined by those who have tackled Combe Hill.)

Take a breather to admire the stunning panorama spread below along the valley. On a clear day you should be able to see the outskirts of Northampton, Ecton, Earls Barton, Great Doddington and the woodland of Irchester Country Park. Even more is revealed as you move around this isolated plateau.

There is no road to the church, only the footpath and a track over the far boundary wall that leads to a tarmac path. Castle Ashby House can be seen among the distant trees. Carry on down the hill and up again to Castle Ashby, which you enter at the side of The Falcon Hotel, opposite the war memorial. If you choose to linger here awhile, stay on the narrow lane as there is plenty to see. The elegant house

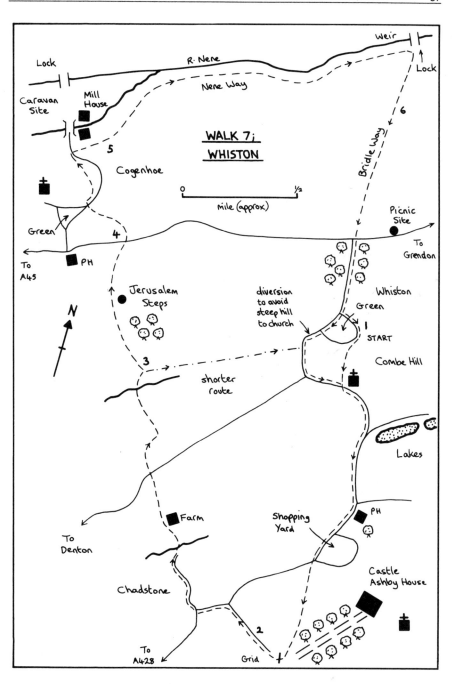

Weir

Lock

R. Nene

Nene Way

Lock

Caravan Site

Mill House

WALK 7;
WHISTON

6

Bridle Way

5

Cogenhoe

0        ½

mile (approx)

Picnic Site

To Grendon

Green

4

To A45

PH

Jerusalem Steps

N

diversion to avoid steep hill to church

Whiston Green

START

1

Combe Hill

3

shorter route

Lakes

To Denton

Farm

Shopping Yard

PH

Castle Ashby House

Chadstone

2

To A428

Grid

(now a conference centre) set in private grounds is attributed to Capability Brown. The church of St Mary Magdalene and the adjacent Orangery and gardens are open to the public all year round. Yet a further tempting option is the Shopping Yard, with a café and other attractions to lure the passer-by!

Back to the road! On the bend out of the village, a finger-post leads across toward the broad avenue of mature trees which sweeps down from the façade of the house and fades away over the hill.

**2.** Turn right out of the park over the cattle-grid then proceed to the T-junction. Go briefly left to the hamlet of Chadstone. Go on to the outlying farm, where the bridleway takes you over the horizon to cross the Whiston to Denton road, and on down to the wooden bridge over the brook.

**3.** It is possible to take a shorter route back to Whiston at this point as indicated on the map.

**4.** Otherwise, if you are keeping to the longer route, go up the slope. Only a few metres into the woodland, find the short flight of steps in the steep bank, perhaps hidden in summer by the branches and foliage. Emerge to the field edge (and several waymarks) to go straight ahead to the Jerusalem Steps (also known as Hallelujah Steps). The level changes are a result of past quarrying. Pass between a double hedgerow as you go down to the road on the perimeter of Cogenhoe.

Almost opposite, a sign indicates the line through to the village green. Now joining the Nene Way, the path slips between a high wall and houses, seemingly a dead end. However, this soon opens up to Church Field.

Before the Mill House and caravan park, observe the Nene Way discs beside a private garage and stay on the riverside to Whiston Lock, a popular swimming hole earlier in the century. Watch out for the elusive kingfisher in this quiet backwater.

**5.** Leave the water and turn sharp right in sight of the church tower at Whiston. On the road, take note of a plaque on a stone plinth to commemorate the replanting of an avenue of trees 'to mark the Silver Jubilee of Queen Elizabeth II, unveiled by Earl Compton 7 June 1977'.

# Castle Ashby

Castle Ashby is one of the great houses of Northamptonshire. It is of the Elizabethan and Jacobean periods, and the ancestral home of the Marquess of Northampton. Although the house of Weldon stone, fine terraces and the immediate park landscaped by Capability Brown are not generally open to the public, the splendid 10 hectares (25 acres) of the adjacent gardens are open all year round. These include an arboretum, orangery and lakes.

Sir William Compton was a lawyer and personal friend of Henry VIII. He started to build the house in 1574 on the site of an old, ruined castle. Over the next 150 years his descendants made additions. A remarkable feature of the mansion is the carved Latin text cut into the balustrade of the parapet, which translates as follows: 'Except the Lord build the house, they labour in vain who build it.'

There is a romantic story concerning an elopement connected with the Compton family. Although it might be of doubtful authenticity, it is a fact that the heiress voluntarily and daringly abducted by the Compton suitor brought him great riches.

Sir John Spencer was a very wealthy merchant in the City of London, who lived in an impressive house in Islington called Canonbury. Sir John had an only daughter, Elizabeth, who was a lovely slim girl, with brown eyes and hair, and jealously guarded by her father against her many suitors. Elizabeth, however, had her own ideas. She had fallen in love with William Compton of Castle Ashby, who returned her affections and was determined to marry her. John Spencer did not share their views and did everything within his power to keep them apart, even keeping his daughter a virtual prisoner. He wanted her to marry a rich, eligible man of business instead of Sir William, whose family was not particularly wealthy at that time.

Regardless of this, William was an extremely persistent suitor and devised an ingenious plan to rescue his beloved from the clutches of her father. He disguised himself as a baker's boy to gain access to Canonbury House. Compton carried a great basket of loaves, which he left in the kitchen, and proceeded to smuggle Elizabeth out of the house concealed in the bulky carrier!

The couple eloped and the rich merchant was so utterly incensed at the match that he refused to have anything to do with his daughter and her new husband, or even to acknowledge his baby grandson. The estrangement might have gone on for years, except that the Queen decided to take the matter in hand. She asked Sir John if he would sponsor a protégé of hers who had been disowned by his parents, to which he readily agreed, not wishing to upset his monarch.

The Court proceeded to the Queen's private chapel, where the baby's baptism was to take place. Her Majesty gave the boy the name of Spencer. The godfather was so enamoured of the infant that he promised to make his namesake his sole heir. A great surprise was revealed to the old man when the Queen sent for the child's parents. Lord Compton led his wife, whose eyes were red with weeping, into the royal presence. Throwing herself at her father's feet, Elizabeth begged for his forgiveness, backed by her loyal husband. To the astonishment of John Spencer the Queen instructed him 'to take the parents back into your favour and forgive them, for the child you have adopted is your own grandson'.

The merchant became reconciled to his daughter's marriage, and when he died in 1610 left her his great fortune, which was estimated to be worth £300,000. Lord Compton was said to be quite unhinged for a time with so much wealth and consequently, the Lord Chamberlain had to take his affairs in hand. This was not the case for Elizabeth, for she knew the power of money and how to apply it. She told her spouse that she required £16,000 per annum for her apparel and £600 for charitable works. She insisted upon six to eight gentlemen attendants, four footmen etc., £800 for jewels and £2,000 for her purse. Lord Compton was made the Earl of Northampton by James I.

# Walk 8: Litchborough

## Litchborough – Church Stowe – Upper Stowe – Litchborough

**Distance:** 5 miles

**Terrain:** Hilly

**Starting Point:** The crossroads on the B4525 in Litchborough GR 633642

**Map:** OS Landranger 152 Northampton

---

**1.** From the crossroads (B4525) in Litchborough, walk down the Farthingstone road to the last house, where a recessed gate, stile and finger-post indicate your path. It is clearly marked.

Once over the hump of the hill and the hefty bridge, the path becomes quite steep as you head for a lone tree on the skyline. This circuit is highly recommended for its sylvan scenery, being a part of the Northamptonshire Uplands. Its beauty is ample compensation for the extra effort involved!

Over the crest, keep to a diagonal line into the dip to skirt Waterloo Barn. Then head up again to the Stowe road. Cross the brow of the hill to the lane, where there is a seat from which to contemplate this rolling 'champagne country'.

In Church Stowe (Stowe-Nine-Churches), allow time to wander round to the south side to absorb the view over Weedon and beyond. Enter St Michael's Church under the Norman arch of the north door, if only to wonder at the exquisite and elegantly carved figure of Lady Elizabeth Carey who died in 1630 (she married the Earl of Danby). The neck ruff of her gown, the lining of her cloak and the ornate pillow are, in themselves, intricate works of art. The monument is by Nicholas Stone, master mason to Charles I.

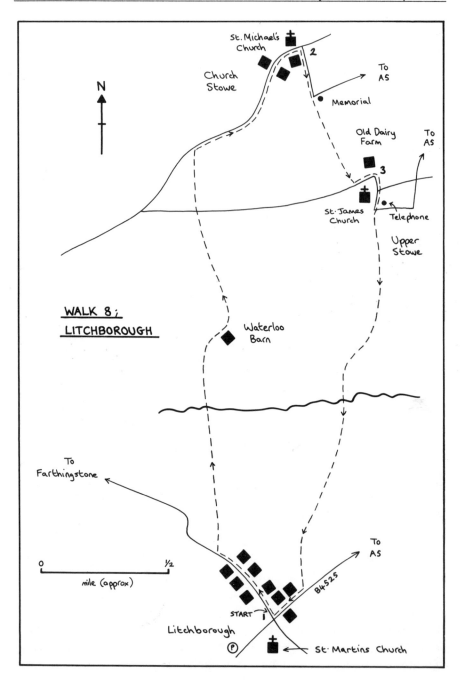

N

St. Michael's
Church

2

Church
Stowe

To
AS

Memorial

Old Dairy
Farm

To
AS

3

St. James
Church

Telephone

Upper
Stowe

WALK 8 ;
LITCHBOROUGH

Waterloo
Barn

To
Farthingstone

0                          ½

mile (approx)

To
AS

B4525

START

Litchborough

Ⓟ

St. Martins Church

Another outstanding monument is of a cross-legged Knight, Sir Gerard de L'isle, circa. 1287. Fashioned in Purbeck marble and clad in a detailed tunic over chain mail, he reposes with a delicately pointed foot.

**2.** Wind through the street of delightful dwellings as far as the war memorial and seat, then descend sharply over the compact little valley to Upper Stowe.

**3.** Go left at the road, next to Old Dairy Farm (craft centre and teas). Over the way, St James's, a chapel of ease, stands apart among the trees as the route passes by, to the curve of the lane.

A gap to the left of the (slightly misleading) finger-post leads through a plantation in the dip, before once again rising 'up hill and down dale'. A number of waymarks, pursue a slanting trail.

On the return approach to Litchborough, leave the fields to join the B4525 at the crossroads.

A visit to St Matthew's Church may be rewarded with the sight of a rare stained-glass sundial high up in one of the windows and five scratch-dials, for which a search is necessary. On the outside look up to the stone heads over the north door, where one face appears to register alarm! Two hatchments of the gentry, high on the wall, display their coats of arms.

## Stowe-Nine-Churches

The Stowes occupy high ground overlooking a panorama of sweeping countryside. Stowe Church and Upper Stowe lie to the west of Watling Street (A5). Upper Stowe used to be called Butter Stowe because a carrier from London collected butter from the local farms. These two villages make up the parish of Stowe-Nine-Churches. There are various theories as to how the name of Stowe-Nine-Churches came about: that nine churches may be seen from the parish of Stowe, or that in the reign of Henry VII, the Lord of the Manor had the right of presentations to nine local churches. The latter is perhaps the most likely explanation. The most interesting tale, though, is the legend about the Saxon church.

The monk blessed the tired serfs and sent them on their way after the day's work. He had been telling them a simple parable from the bible, but his audience had been inattentive, and the holy man realised that they wanted to get home and rest from their labours. All day they had been toiling on the strips of ploughed land. What was really needed in Stowe, was a church in which he could preach the word of God. They needed the shelter from the wind and rain, instead of listening to him under the open sky in all weathers.

The monk looked up at the castle on the hill, where the Thane of Stowe resided. In a flash of inspiration he decided to ask the thane for his help in building a church for the village. The nobleman and the holy man sat by the blazing log fire in the castle and discussed the idea. The thane was amenable to the monk's suggestion and it was decided to build the church in the valley below the village.

Work proceeded the next day, with the digging out of the trenches for the foundations. To the dismay of the labourers and masons, when they arrived at the site the following morning the trenches had been filled in. The men worked with determination to clear the holes again and to lay the stone for the walls. Well pleased with their efforts, they went home for the night. Yet the following day, not only were the trenches filled with soil, but also the stones had been scattered about the vale. The monk stood by mystified, and watched the men restart the digging. He was angry and could not understand why the new church should be constantly vandalised.

The same destruction took place seven times overnight and the labourers became sullen and resentful. It took all his powers of persuasion for the monk to urge the men to have another try at the construction of the holy place. The monk suggested that this time someone should watch through the night, but no one wanted to stay behind alone, as they were frightened of the unseen. After some deliberation, one brave man volunteered, and the holy man visited him after dark to ensure that all was well.

The band of men arrived on the site very early the following morning, and to their horror the damage had occurred again. However, no harm appeared to have befallen the volunteer, although he did have a very strange tale to relate. All had been well until midnight, when a dark shape appeared over the brow of the hill. He could not see clearly, as there was no moon, but he said, 'It was a crettar no bigger nor a hog.' It had moved quickly and silently, and seemed to be so strong that it picked up the heavy stones without any effort and hurled them about the valley, then filled the trenches with soil. The creature only ceased when the cock crowed and the day had dawned, when it had run off over the hill!

The labourers were astonished to hear the news and all began to speak at once. They thought it was Beelzebub, or the Devil himself, but the commanding voice of the monk silenced them. He told them it was nothing of the kind, but a messenger from God, who had been sent to make them understand that they had started to build the church in the wrong place. 'We must start again, but this time it must be high on a hilltop, where the villagers from miles around will see the tower and hear the bell.'

So, for the ninth and last time, they renewed their efforts on a hill overlooking Weedon. It was to be a simple edifice, with a fine Saxon tower. According to the legend, this was how the parish of Stowe-Nine-Churches came by its name.

There are many churches built on a hill in this country, and dedicated to St Michael. Several of these have a similar legend in regard to the disputed site. St Michael could be said to be the obvious choice for a saint to oppose the Devil in high places, as it was he who threw Lucifer out of heaven.

## The Old Red Lion, Litchborough

Litchborough has a long history that goes back beyond Norman times, but an unusual folk tale is far more recent. It is connected with The Old Red Lion inn, which stands opposite St Martin's Church and the modest green, and is said to have taken place in the 19th century.

On a cold November morning, before it was light, the gravedigger went into the churchyard to inspect a corner of the cemetery where he was due to dig a grave that day. As he walked down the gravel path he almost fell over the prone body of a man, which was slumped across a mound of earth where a villager had been buried the previous day. The workman turned the body over and noted that the man had been dead for some hours. He recognised the fellow as George Bates, who had been a regular customer at The Old Red Lion. The doctor was summoned to examine the corpse, and pronounced the cause of death as a heart attack. The strange thing was that George's face was contorted with fear. He was also clutching a sword with both hands. The sword had been plunged through his tailcoat and into the soil.

It was a complete mystery until a group of cronies who drank at the pub revealed an incident that had taken place in the tavern the previous night. They had been gathered round the blazing log fire in the tap room, supping their porter and smoking their pipes, when the conversation had turned to the subject of old Albert's funeral that had taken place that very day, which the majority had attended. They said that he had been a fine man who would be missed in the village. Suddenly, up jumped George Bates, who had been drinking heavily all night. He said that they were 'a lot of hypocrites' and that old Albert had been a miserable old codger. The company was aghast at his words and told him that it was unlucky to deride a person's character after death, but George was unrepentant and stated that he would say as much to his face, if he were still alive.

A sword had been hanging over the fireplace of the inn for many years, and a local joker called Nobby Clark dared George to plunge it in old Albert's freshly dug grave. In a show of bravado, he took up the challenge and removed the sword from the wall. His mates guided him across the road to the churchyard and left him by the grave. It was a stormy night and the drinkers were glad to return to the warmth of the tavern. What a fool George was, they chuntered to themselves, to wander about the churchyard in the dead of night.

For many weeks the strange death of George Bates was the chief topic of discussion in The Old Red Lion. When the inebriated group of friends had left their comrade by the grave of old Albert on that wet November night, they had presumed that he would not actually carry out the silly act, but have the sense to go home instead. However, he must have taken the dare seriously, and tried to plunge the sword into the mound, not realising that he had inadvertently speared his tailcoat as well. When he had struggled to get up, he must have found himself well and truly pinned down. In his befuddled state of mind, he might have imagined that old Albert had reached out from the grave to take his revenge. The opinion in the pub was that George Bates had died of a heart attack brought on by fear, which accounted for the horrified expression on his face.

No matter what sort of a character a person had, be they good, bad or indifferent, after death, only good things were to be said about the departed. It was believed that 'no good comes of speaking ill of the dead'. Churchyards have always been awe-inspiring places, and graves have always been treated with reverence. To walk over a grave or to disturb it in any way was considered to be not only disrespectful, but also unlucky.

# Walk 9: Boughton

*Boughton Obelisk (optional) – Boughton – Pitsford –*
*Moulton – Boughton Green – Boughton*

**Distance:** Complete circuit about 7 miles. Shorter route (omitting Moulton) 5 miles.

**Terrain:** Gently rolling countryside

**Starting Point:** Boughton Obelisk GR 754654 or Humfrey Lane, Boughton village GR 753659. Shorter route GR 767668

**Map:** OS Pathfinder 978 Northampton North and Long Buckby SP66/76

**1. If you choose to begin this walk at the obelisk**, leave Northampton on the A508 to Market Harborough Road. Turn right at the cemetery into Boughton Green Road and then first left into Obelisk Drive, which you follow to the monument. Built by William Wentworth, 7th Earl of Strafford, in 1764, the 100ft column of local white sandstone was the most prominent of the seven follies within the confines of Boughton Park. Sadly, few of the originals remain and none of the others is open for public view.

It was erected 'in memory of His Grace William Cavendish, 4th Duke of Devonshire' who became Prime Minister in 1756 and was a close friend of Wentworth. Today it stands on a rather forlorn green sward, almost swallowed by a housing estate. There are no signs to indicate the way through to Boughton village, so choose an opening on the lower side of the spinney. The short path filters into the elegant ambience of Spinney Close and goes on to an extremely tidy path, ending adjacent to a bus stop in Humfrey Lane. Note the fine iron gates of Ashley House, the pretty cottage with the rounded stone wall and the village signpost. If preferred, **the walk may be started at this central point in Boughton village**, excluding the Obelisk.

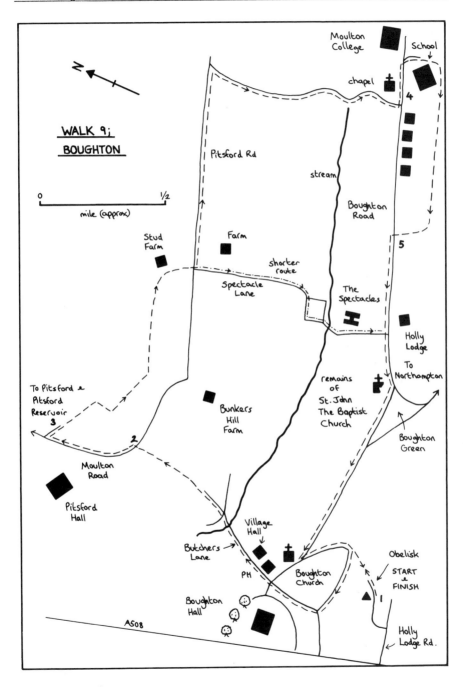

N

WALK 9;
BOUGHTON

0 _____ ½
mile (approx)

Moulton College

School

chapel

4

Pitsford Rd

stream

Boughton Road

5

Stud Farm

Farm

shorter route

Spectacle Lane

The Spectacles

Holly Lodge

To Northampton

To Pitsford & Pitsford Reservoir
3

2

Bunkers Hill Farm

remains of St. John The Baptist Church

Boughton Green

Moulton Road

Pitsford Hall

Village Hall

Butchers Lane

PH

Boughton Hall

A508

Boughton Church

Obelisk

START & FINISH

1

Holly Lodge Rd.

At the meeting of the ways, the imposing gateway to Boughton Hall is on the rise. The square-towered church of St John the Baptist is in Church Street, next to the Whyte Melville public house. This gentleman was a local philanthropist and writer of sporting publications, who donated his royalties to the less fortunate of the sporting fraternity and founded the Working Men's Club in Northampton.

The ubiquitous chestnut tree rises from a raised stone ring, with seats echoing the circle. Just below are the Village Hall and a spring on the verge that is said never to have run dry in living memory. Wizard topiary catches the eye then shortly the lane narrows and you catch a glimpse of rolling parkland. Bunkers Hill Farm lies ahead, as the finger-post points away over the hill, on a stretch of permitted path. Note, however, that tour route does not go to the farm. Look back to see only the tall chimneys of the hall, barely distinguishable from the treetops.

**2.** The stark lines of the Obelisk remain an eye-catcher along much of this walk. Leave the path to join the road and carry on to Pitsford, passing the gates of Pitsford Hall, the premises of the Northamptonshire Grammar School. An exploration of Pitsford may be favoured – Grange Lane is central for the bus stop, phone box, shop and pub. Further down this lane there is ample car parking at Pitsford Reservoir, with extensive views from the choice picnic site.

**3.** To continue the circuit, turn back into Moulton Road and proceed to the curve of the hill, where dwellings are slightly set back and a post directs the walker to stay beside the fence for a mile or so, by-passing the stud farm on your way to the road.

*For the shorter walk, excluding Moulton, go straight over to Spectacle Lane at this point. Walk the entire length of the lane and rejoin the longer route on Boughton Road. You will see the twin turrets of The Spectacles, the fascinating folly built at the behest of the 2nd Earl of Strafford in the late 18th century.*

To continue the main walk after reaching the road after the stud farm, find a path just in Spectacle Lane. The path runs by the narrow spinney and parallel to the Moulton road to finish on the hill opposite the environs of Moulton College.

**4.** Continue to a left turn by Carey Baptist Church. Nearby, high on the wall, a plaque records that in this cottage lived William Carey 1785-1789, the dedicated missionary who was buried at Serampure, India. The Telegraph pub abuts this wall, all in close proximity to the respected agricultural establishment, Moulton College. Cross to Pound Lane to note the small disc on the gate of Moulton School. The path winds through its grounds and along the back gardens of houses.

**5.** After four fields (and slightly awkward double stiles) make for the road to Boughton Green. Almost immediately the unique implement gate of Holly Lodge comes into sight, and the interesting façade of panels embellished with cherubs. The shorter route rejoins at the junction with Spectacle Lane.

Walk on to the dip, where the abandoned remains of the old church of St John the Baptist lie in a dismal, neglected corner. These pathetic ruins, though picturesque, are only saved from total collapse by the sinuous ropes of the smothering and prolific ivy. Only a trace of the former holy well is visible. It was believed to have had healing properties. Stories abound of ghosts of both sexes, seen at midnight on Christmas Eve, who beckoned folk with promises – and led them to death! From here carry on to Boughton to finish the walk.

## Boughton Green

The crumbling walls of the church of St John the Baptist lie adjacent to Boughton Green, half a mile from the present village of Boughton. The tower and spire toppled in 1785, some 200 years after the last service was conducted there. The healing spring of St John is now almost hidden among the debris of the fallen stones, but was greatly revered in medieval times. It was the tradition that clergymen came from six miles around to pray and preach for an hour on St John the Baptist Day. Afterwards, the local youths played football and indulged in other pastimes until tradesmen set up their colourful booths to cater for the gathering. These modest beginnings were to become the annual Boughton Green Fair.

## Boughton Green Ghost Story

The overgrown churchyard of the ruined church of St John is haunted by a strange ghost which seems to display a dual personality! Sometimes it appears as a handsome young man, at other times a beautiful girl. This sinister spirit manifests itself to passers-by on Christmas Eve and lures them to an untimely end by extracting a kiss from each unsuspecting victim.

Many hundreds of years ago, when the church was still in good repair, a local girl from Boughton married her fiancé on Christmas Eve. They could have lived a long and happy life together, but disaster struck the couple when, only after a month of wedded bliss, the young husband died of a mysterious illness. His bride was so distraught that she returned to the graveyard and committed suicide. At that time, a person who committed suicide could not be buried in consecrated ground, and consequently, she was placed in a grave outside the cemetery wall.

Legend has it that if a woman passes this isolated spot on Christmas Eve, the ghost appears as the bridegroom and demands a kiss and a promise to meet him in the churchyard a month later. The female fails to keep the tryst, as she invariably dies within the month. Should the late night traveller be a man, the apparition will materialise before the unsuspecting male as the bride. She makes the same request to meet a month hence at that very spot, kisses him on the lips and then vanishes. The same fate awaits the bewildered man!

In one version of the tale it is recorded that in 1875 a farmer by the name of William Parker was trudging home that way at midnight on Christmas Eve. To his astonishment he saw a beautiful young woman sitting on the churchyard wall wearing a flimsy white gown. He wondered what on earth she was thinking of to be dallying in that lonely place at so late an hour and to be so lightly clad on a perishing winter's night. She called the farmer over and asked if he would meet her there in a month's time. He readily agreed to her request, but before he could ask any questions she pressed her cold lips on his and ran swiftly away, her shoes making no sound on the gravel path. William shivered involuntarily as he went on his way feeling utterly despondent. He realised that he had had an encounter with the notorious Boughton ghost. According to local lore he died a month later, on the 24th January 1876.

## Boughton Green Fair

Boughton Green Fair was once a thriving source of pleasure and entertainment in these parts. A horse market was a popular feature of this annual event, drawing villagers from miles around. On the triangular piece of ground adjoining the now desolate church of St John the Baptist, one of the most important horse fairs in the Midlands was to develop. Edward III granted a Charter for the fair at Boughton in 1351. It took place on the 24th June and continued for the two succeeding days. The first day was given over to the selling of wooden ware of every kind, and on the second day the local gentry came to watch the horse racing and wrestling. Following these events there were exhibitions of curiosities, menageries and theatricals. The stalls, shows and bright swings attracted the younger element, whilst their elders were drawn to the fortune-tellers or paid the pipers in the dancing tents. Itinerant traders sold all manner of wares made in the surrounding towns and villages. Cakes from Banbury, rakes from Corby and Geddington, and carved artefacts and spoons from King's Cliffe. The third day was given over to the prime business of selling horses, ponies and sheep.

The large amounts of money that passed hands at this popular event also attracted the criminal fraternity. An affray took place in the 19th century when a gang of thieves led by an individual who styled himself 'Captain Slash' descended on the fair at night. The marauding mob released some of the animals from the Wild Beast Show and stole money from the sleeping stallholders. In the darkness, all was chaos for a time, with the noise of the terrified beasts, plus the screams and shouts of the rudely awakened showmen and vendors. One quick-witted booth-holder, a Mrs Dickens, managed to tie her moneybags around her waist under her nightclothes and run all the way home to Northampton, a distance of three and a half miles!

The indignant fairground folk eventually overcame the band of ruffians. Along with their leader, George Catherall, a Lancashire prizefighter, the gang was carted off to the county gaol. Catherall was sentenced to death, the ultimate penalty, but before he was hanged on the 21st July 1826, he threw off his boots. He did this to make liars, he said, of those who prophesised that he would die with them on!

# Walk 10: Sulgrave to Eydon

## *Sulgrave – Culworth – Eydon*

**Distance:** 3½ miles, linear. *Be prepared to walk back unless you have a car at each end!*

**Terrain:** Very hilly

**Starting Point:** The stocks, Sulgrave GR 558453

**Map:** OS Landranger 152 Northampton

This linear walk is set in the Northamptonshire Uplands in the south-west of the county. Consequently, there are several fairly steep hills and some irksome stiles. The village of Eydon is on a rise of 580ft. Sulgrave is reached by taking the A43 north from Brackley to turn off at High Cross just before the village of Syresham onto the B4525. The village is 7 miles further on.

**1.** Sulgrave is perhaps best known for the manor, ancestral home of George Washington. Hâve a look at the stocks and whipping post in the main street before crossing to Stockwell Lane and following the bridleway to emerge at the junction with the road to Culworth. Walk up this road as far as the village sign, where a finger-post points the way to the centre.

**2.** A gate beside St Mary's Church gives public access to a County Heritage Site at Bury Hill, a scheduled Ancient Monument known as Culworth Castle. It is a massive ringwork of the fortified site and stands surrounded by a well-defined ditch or moat (2 metres deep and 6 metres wide) in a field called Bury Close. An information board tells that King William 'caused castles to be built which were a sore burden to the poor' (taken from an Anglo-Saxon chronicle of AD1086). In that year the land was held by Landrick of Gilo.

Continue on this little diversion to The Manor House, facing the green. Against the wall lies Charlie's Pebble. This hefty boulder is said to have been the one on which Charles I stood to review his amassed army of 10,000 troops before the Battle of Cropredy Bridge. A local loyal supporter had entertained him, and his visit was documented in June 1644, en route to the ensuing clash.

A curious, stone 'chair' stands on the green. It is believed to have been in use as the auctioneer's seat, and was previously mounted on the base of the original cross over the road, which was converted to the war memorial. There was probably a market held here as from the 17th century, drove roads, both from Scotland and Wales, criss-crossed the county. Cattle were herded on foot until the trade was transferred to the railways. One such important drove route, the Welsh road, ran directly through Culworth and on to Buckingham. Often after the long trek cattle were temporarily halted and fattened on local grazing before ultimately being offered for sale in the bigger towns.

**3.** Carry on down the hill to Paddocks Farm where, on the other side of the road to the farm, a finger-post shows the way beside a stone wall. This opens to hilly terrain. At the time of writing, the brick bridge over the dismantled railway line is in a dangerous state and a minor diversion is marked and recommended. In its heyday, the Great Central Line was an important link crossing the county between Brackley and to the north of Kilsby.

After the next stile strike out at an angle, going midfield over the rump of the hill and making for a gap in the hedge close to two tall trees. Go straight on to Ashpole Spinney in the dip.

Bear slightly left here into the next field and down to cross the brook, then up again into Eydon Park. Here there is a view of Eydon Hall, built for The Reverend Francis Annesley in 1789-91. As the driveway curves toward the buildings, veer away to the right past the pond and duck-house, heading towards the church of St Nicholas and through the iron kissing gate.

The lichen-covered walls enclose the path leading to the green, where the stocks and whipping-post were set up alongside the vil-

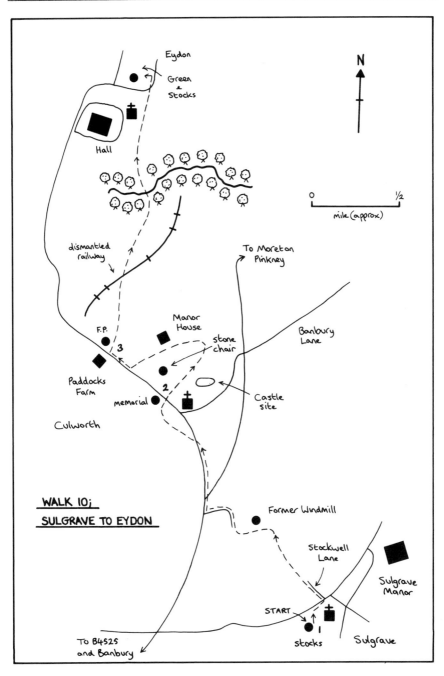

Eydon

Green
&
Stocks

Hall

N

0        ½
mile (approx)

dismantled
railway

To Moreton
Pinkney

Manor
House

F.P.

3

stone
chair

Banbury
Lane

Paddocks
Farm

2

memorial

Castle
site

Culworth

WALK 10;
SULGRAVE TO EYDON

Former Windmill

Stockwell
Lane

Sulgrave
Manor

START

stocks

Sulgrave

To B4525
and Banbury

lage pump in 1828, at a cost of £6 15s 6d. North Lodge gatehouse has a niche hung with a fire bell over the door.

The Royal Oak public house is in Lime Avenue (The 'Back'), a section of the rectangle on which this orderly village is based and where many of the dwellings are now listed buildings in the neat Conservation Area. Two major fires here in August 1651 and 1905 wreaked considerable havoc to both property and produce, ultimately causing great changes to the face of the community.

## Culworth

Culworth lies in the south-west corner of the county, seven miles from Banbury. At the end of the 18th century this small community was the headquarters for a band of thieves numbering around fifteen men at the height of their activities. They were the scourge of a large area of Northamptonshire and the neighbouring counties of Oxfordshire and Warwickshire. Culworth was a remote village at that time, highly, suited to the criminal purpose of the fraternity. The geographical position of the place also provided the main escape routes – Banbury Lane and Welsh Lane, the two ancient drove tracks that passed through Culworth. The busy turnpike road which bisected Whittlebury Forest carried a lot of traffic between Oxford and Northampton, thus attracting the attentions of the Culworth gang and becoming the setting for a host of insidious acts of highway robbery.

Their leader was John Smith, who was described as being a strong and daring character. His two sons were also involved. Four labourers, Bowers, Malmsbury, Turrell and a local man, John Tack, also joined the brotherhood. Another important member was William Abbott, who came from nearby Sulgrave, a seemingly respectable resident of the community, who was both a shoemaker and parish clerk. However, he always carried pistols, even in church, and used to hide their ill-gotten gains within the place of worship!

The gang started off in a small way with poaching, but this soon led to more extreme crimes. They were efficient and thorough in their exploits, although, by modern standards, they were not vicious, for they were never known to have killed anyone. One of their most brutal attacks was on a Mr Wyatt, a farmer from Sulgrave. They knocked him to the ground and battered him about before dragging the man into the house, where they locked him and his wife into the pantry. The thieves then proceeded to steal money and goods to the value of £40. Eventually their luck ran out when two of the ruffians, Richard Law and William Pettifer, became careless and were caught at an inn in Towcester. They told the landlord that the bags contained fighting cocks. After the two men had retired to bed, the innkeeper became suspicious and opened one of the sacks. When he discovered two masks and smock frocks he sent for the constable. The officer advised the landlord to say nothing to the culprits, and the next morning Law and Pettifer were allowed to leave as normal. A few days later, another burglary took place at a farm, where the robbers were seen to be wearing masks and smocks. This was the clue for which the constable had been waiting, and he then revealed the information discovered by himself and the landlord to the authorities.

Law and Pettifer were arrested but denied any knowledge of the crime, which was not surprising as it had been committed by other members of the gang, led by Bowers. Hoping to save their own necks, they impeached Bowers and the rest of the mob, confessing to many more crimes over the past decade.

The criminals were duly arrested and sent for trial at

Northampton Assizes in 1787. Five of the deviants, John Smith senior, Richard Law, William Pettifer, William Bowers and William Abbott, were given the death sentence. The latter was subsequently reprieved and transported to Australia, for life. An excited crowd of 5,000 gathered on Northampton Heath to watch the public execution when, at midday on 3rd August 1787, the four leaders of the Culworth gang were 'launched into eternity'. After suffering a decade of terror in the countryside around the villages, the ordinary folk of the area could, at last, sleep safe and sound in their beds under the dark veil of night!

## Sulgrave

The beautiful brownstone Tudor building of Sulgrave Manor dates back to the 16th century, when it was the ancestral home of the Washington family. They lived in the manor house from 1540 to 1657. Lawrence Washington is recognised as the founder of the Sulgrave Washingtons. Lawrence purchased the manor of Sulgrave from the Crown in 1538. He was married twice. His first wife died in childbirth and his second spouse, Amy Thomson, bore him eleven children. He probably had the mansion built to accommodate his expanding family. His wool stapling business flourished and he twice became Mayor of Northampton, ultimately dying a wealthy man.

It was the wool merchant's two-times great-grandson, Colonel John Washington, who emigrated to America in 1656, to settle in Virginia. His great-grandson, George Washington, born in 1732, was to become the first President of the United States. In the spandrel of the main doorway the Washington coat of arms may be seen. It consists of three mullets and two bars, these emblems thought to be the original Stars and Stripes of the American national flag.

The manor at Sulgrave had deteriorated to the state of a dilapidated farmhouse in the 1890s, when a body of British subscribers purchased it. It was presented to the peoples of America and Britain to celebrate 100 years of peace and friendship between the two countries.

# Walk 11: King's Cliffe

## *King's Cliffe – Fineshade Abbey – Blatherwycke – King's Cliffe*

**Distance:** 8 miles

**Terrain:** Undulating, rural

**Starting Point:** Memorial pillar, Law's Lane, King's Cliffe GR 006917

**Map:** OS Pathfinders 917 Corby North and Uppingham SP89/99, and 918 Peterborough South and Wansford TL09/19

---

**1.** The church of All Saints and St James stands in isolation and is the pivot of this 'up hill and down dale' walk. A stone memorial pillar and a modern phone box are to one side of Law's Lane.

Turn left and uphill, opposite The Cross Keys, into West Street, which is bordered by elegant stone houses, many swathed with creeper.

**2.** At the fork with the Blatherwycke road, cross over to Wood Lane and go over the bridge of the former railway line, then immediately left on the field edge.

**3.** On your right is Westhay Wood, and the trees appear to get closer as the next fields become more hemmed in on both sides. A stile gives access to the wood. Keep forward, to brush past a cutting of the defunct line (ignore the unsafe bridge nearby) and to continue beside a tatty iron fence. Briefly enter a clearing and then the open field.

Keep to the perimeter until a path cuts diagonally across the big field to enter Lynn Wood. At the track, bear right to exit at the gate. Here the vista broadens to Wakerley Wood, which covers the horizon on the far ridge. Among the trees are the angular lines of Laxton Hall. A little lower down, the A43 to Stamford resembles a busy belt with moving traffic.

Directly in front, but partially hidden by the brow of the hill, is Fineshade Abbey. Once the site of St. Mary's priory and Hymel Castle. The late 18th-century stable block has been converted to residential use.

**4.** The worn path drops away to the left, and a backward glance reveals extensive earthworks of the early castle/abbey site and a better view of the house. The surrounding fence to the property has an access stile to the Jurassic Way, which goes on to Top Lodge, the offices of the Forestry Commission and a caravan site.

In the hollow, go over the stile against the fence then four fields. Exit at the lane to Wakerley, near to Home Farm at Blatherwycke.

On this protracted slope a sweeping panorama unfolds. Thick skeins of trees ripple over the landscape, giving a delightful overview of the huge lake and the peeping rooftops of the village ahead.

Stroll through this quiet place. Look over the parapet of the long bridge to see the Staffordshire knot, the emblem of the influential Staffords, who were formerly in residence at Blatherwycke Hall. Now only the lodge gates mark the entrance to the park.

**5.** On the bend of Lowick Road, at the top of the hill, swing left at a finger-post to Blatherwycke Church and in front of a stone barn whose roof is dotted with mosses like faded velvet pincushions.

Keep strictly to the footpath (except perhaps for a side visit to the church) and do not miss the somewhat incongruous figure of Apollo Belvedere, who stands on a pedestal, quite alone and abandoned, in a wide, open field. He is a forlorn reminder of the former glory of the gardens of Blatherwycke Hall. (Please note that there is no public right of way for a closer inspection!) Carry on, with glimpses of Blatherwycke Lake through the greenery. The great hall has long since vanished. Coming to Alders Farm, cross straight over next to a brick barn, then walk down beside Willow Brook.

King's Cliffe is sighted after the footbridge, as the path slides past the allotments to the mellowed stone wall of The Maltings. Clipping the

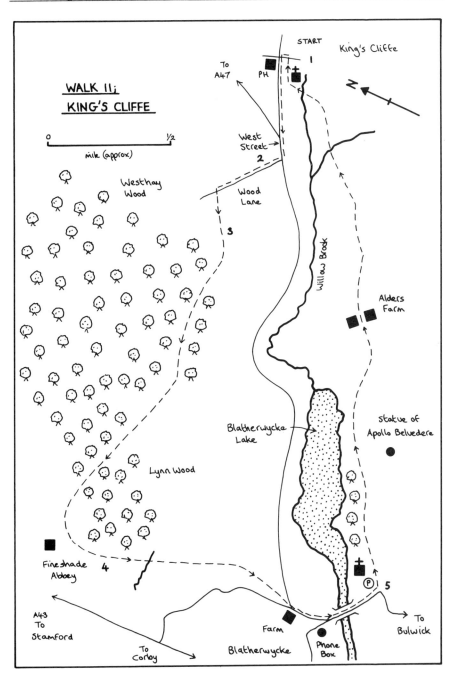

WALK 11;
KING'S CLIFFE

0 _____ ½
mile (approx)

START

King's Cliffe

To
A47

PH

1

West
Street

2

Wood
Lane

3

Westhay
Wood

Willow Brook

Alders
Farm

Statue of
Apollo Belvedere

Blatherwycke
Lake

Lynn Wood

Finesthade
Abbey

4

A43
To
Stamford

To
Corby

Farm

Blatherwycke

Phone
Box

P

5

To
Bulwick

pocket park, wander by intriguing little jitties such as Eagles Lane,
Rates Lane and Garden Lane as the shady alleyway rises and curves,
adding a tinge of mystery as to how or where it will end.

All is revealed at the appearance of the 13th-century broach spire as
Church Walk trickles back to the starting point.

## King's Cliffe

King's Cliffe was an important centre of jurisdiction when Rockingham Forest covered the landscape. Most of the older buildings are
built of Collyweston stone and slate. The community was renowned
for the production of wooden utensils by skilled woodturners, using
the wood from the forest, after Henry III, in the 14th century, granted
a charter for a fair and market to be held three days a week. Wooden
spoons, in particular, have retained their popularity and are often
still to be found in local craft shops.

William Law, theologian and historian, was born here in 1686,
the son of a grocer. He was to gain recognition for his religious beliefs and Jacobean leanings, which were not always popular with his
peers. From his tutoring post in London he eventually returned to
his brother's home in King's Cliffe. This was known as 'King John's
Palace' as it had once been a royal manor house. His collection of
books, which he set up as a library, is still referred to by scholars in
his field. He died in April 1761, and was buried beneath a writing
desk tomb in the churchyard.

## Strange Burials at Blatherwycke

Lying in a sheltered dip, almost hidden by wood and water,
Blatherwycke may easily entice the walker to linger longer – the past
haunts one's footsteps at every turn. Blatherwycke Hall was demolished in 1948, after troops in the Second World War left irreparable
damage. Previously, the mansion had stood in splendour by the
lake. Assumed to be the largest man-made lake in the county, it was
dug by Irish labourers who left Ireland at the harrowing time of the
potato famine. The water served the needs of the iron and steelworks
at nearby Corby.

Inside the church of the Holy Trinity, now redundant, are memorials to the Staffords who lived at Blatherwycke Hall for many generations; their emblem was the Staffordshire knot. Another memorial was commissioned by Sir Christopher Hatton, the builder of Kirby Hall. This is to Thomas Randolph, a colleague and poet, who died in 1635, and was carved by Nicholas Stone. The first two lines are:

*'Here sleepeth thirteen! together in one tomb*
*And all these greate, yet quarrel not for roome.'*

In the church is a headstone marking the grave of Anthony Williams, a black servant, who perished at the age of 29 years in 1836 in the act of saving his master from drowning in the lake, although other tales of his demise do exist. The slab, curiously, is set facing the wall, and bears the following inscription:

*'Here a poor wanderer hath found a grave.*
*Who death embraced when struggling with the wave.*
*His home far off in the Indian main,*
*He left to rid himself of slavery's chain.*
*Friendless and comfortless he passed the sea*
*On Albion's shores his search for aye with toiling brow*
*He never found his freedom until now.'*

Another strange burial was discovered in the last century, when two Roman coffins were dug up on glebe land. In the larger coffin, which was over a metre (4ft) long, was the skeleton of a woman, though only from the knees upwards. Close to this coffin was another, only about half a metre (2ft) long, containing the leg bones of the same female and a pale red urn. Why was she buried in this way? The mystery might never been solved, but it has been suggested that this could be the grave of the British Queen Boudicca of the Iceni, who led a failed revolt against the Romans and died in AD62. There is speculation that the queen's resting-place is in Northamptonshire.

# Walk 12: Little Harrowden

## *Little Harrowden – Orlingbury – Pytchley – Little Harrowden*

**Distance:** 12 miles

**Terrain:** Easy

**Starting Point:** School Lane, Little Harrowden GR 872717

**Map:** OS Pathfinder 958 Kettering and Irthingborough SP87/97

---

**1.** The parish of Little Harrowden is the largest in the county and is three-quarters of a mile along the B574, turning west off the main A509 from Wellingborough to Kettering.

Begin at School Lane, in sight of the parish church of St Mary. Go to the primary school and through the playing field. Head for a gate into the field, going down the slope. The square tower of St Mary's Church at Orlingbury is on the rise in front, in gentle countryside and well-cloaked in trees. Over the footbridge, go towards the village, following the path around the edge of the field and the garden fences.

In Rectory Lane, look for a sign against the stone wall by the barn. Pass the village hall before reaching the spread of the green. On the far side, the imposing church with its rose window is worth a visit. You will also see the tomb of Jack of Badsaddle, who, according to legend, killed the last wild wolf in England.

**2.** Turn right by the green and cross over to pass The Queen's Head pub. Just past the pub, turn left at a signpost, which says Bridleway to Pytchley. Follow the sign for the bridleway to Pytchley, keeping to the left hedgerow. When the hedge ends, strike out across the field. At the far side, go left.

Through the gap, keep to the hedge on the left. Pytchley can now be

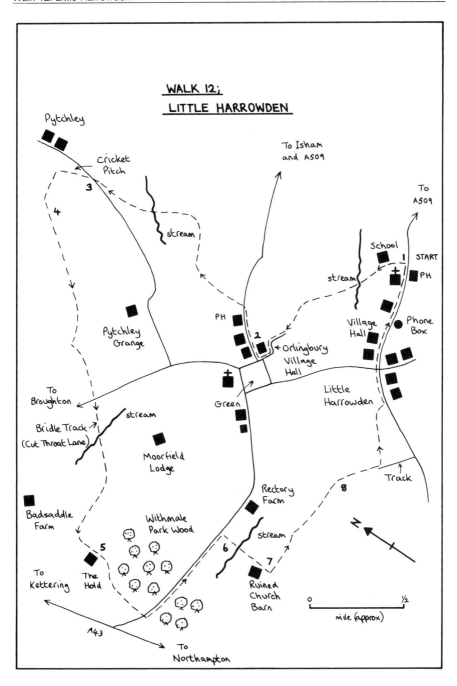

WALK 12;
LITTLE HARROWDEN

Pytchley

Cricket Pitch

3

4

stream

To Isham and A509

To A509

School

START

stream

PH

PH

Village Hall

Phone Box

Pytchley Grange

PH

2

Orlingbury Village Hall

Little Harrowden

To Broughton

Green

Bridle Track (Cut Throat Lane)

stream

Moorfield Lodge

Track

Rectory Farm

8

To Kettering

Badsaddle Farm

Withmale Park Wood

The Hold

5

6

stream

7

Ruined Church Barn

N

A43

To Northampton

0       ½
mile (approx)

seen among the green folds. At the next sign bear right over the field to a dilapidated gate then go down the slope to cross the stile. In the next field, make for a double stile in the meadow. A gate gives access to the lane.

**3.** Turn toward the village for a short distance only. Go on to the cricket field, heading for the barn then keeping straight on to an iron gate beside a water-trough. Keep straight ahead.

**4.** Just before the corner, bear left over the next six fields. At this point in the marker signs become hard to find, keep going until you reach the lane, leading to Broughton. You will arrive at a lane and finger-post. Directly opposite, at the bridleway, proceed between hedges and tall ash trees. This bridle track is known locally as "Cut Throat Lane". Emerging from the tunnel-like footpath, it is almost a relief to see the subtle kaleidoscope of colour of the rolling country-side. Orlingbury church tower may still be seen, and closer still is Moorfield Lodge. The path follows the right hedge and dips down to the stream. Over the bridge, bear slightly to the right, and then left up the hill to the waymark, soon to meet a gravel track. Keep forward to a convergence of the ways at an old gatepost.

**5.** Turn sharp left to a wooden gate and go through a paddock at the rear of a stone house, The Hold. Make doubly sure that the gate is se-curely fastened as there are usually horses grazing here. Keeping to the right hedge, pass Withmale Park Wood. Your route to the road goes via an iron gate and bridleway post indicating the reverse route.

**6.** Turn left along the road for half a mile to a post on the right. Bear diagonally downhill to the wide plank bridge cutting a small corner, then continue to the derelict Harrowden Church Barn.

**7.** Go sharp left and straight across the field towards the corner and a sign on the fence. Join a short. gravel track as you leave the ruined barn behind. Head for a gap in the corner. Little Harrowden now looms into view.

**8.** At the five-fingered post, cross the bridge and turn left, following the village sign to the gravelled track.

**9.** Turn left beneath the electricity pylons, heading for a large opening in the hedge. Go over the field to the dwellings, emerging on the lane and by modern houses. Return to the church and the starting point.

St Mary's Church, Orlingbury

## A Legend of Orlingbury: Jack of Badsaddle

At the heart of the unspoilt village of Orlingbury the large green with its nature trees make it a very pleasant spot. St Mary's Church is opposite and was completely rebuilt in 1843, in the Decorated style of the 14th century. The square tower may be seen for miles around, a fact much appreciated by children as well as their parents, who give permission for them to roam anywhere 'within sight of Orlingbury church'.

In the chancel is the 14th-century alabaster tomb of an armoured knight. On the helmet of the effigy is the inscription 'Nazarini I.H.C'. It is believed to be the tomb of Sir John de Withmayle, whose nickname was Jack of Badsaddle. According to legend, he killed the last wolf in England. Badsaddle is one of Northamptonshire's lost villages, two miles west of Orlingbury, within the parish boundary. Jack is said to have fought the wolf and then a wild boar in the meadow near to his house. After the exhausting encounter, Jack supped at a spring and then died from the effects of gulping the cold water. The source was later named Badsaddle Spring.

The last traces of the tiny, but once thriving hamlet of Withmayle were demolished in 1954. It was a part of a 120-hectare (300-acre estate) owned by Sir John de Withmayle in the reign of King Edward III (1327-1377). Unfortunately, within a few years of taking over the land, the Black Death had wiped out most of the inhabitants. George Vaux, Lord of Great Harrowden, acquired the manor in 1665 and created a park on the estate that remained intact until 1720, by which time only one house from the original community remained.

There is a possibility that Orlingbury means 'Odin's Barrow', for in the Domesday Survey of 1086 it is spelled Ordin Baro. A suggestion lingers that Jack of Orlingbury is really Odin or Wodin the Norse God, who was sometimes portrayed as a famous hunter, a killer of evil beasts. An ancient way once existed between Brixworth and Badsaddle (old Orlingbury). It was called Ash Lane and parts of it can still be seen. The ash was the sacred tree of Odin. Could Ash Lane, therefore, be interpreted as Odin's sacred road?

It is a remarkable coincidence that in these two settlements, Badsaddle and Brixworth, there are two legends relating to the wolf. In Brixworth, Lord Wolfage drives his ghostly carriage at night and stops at Wolfage Bridge. At Badsaddle there is Jack, who kills the wolf. Whatever the explanation, it seems that the myth of Odin made a lasting impression on this part of the county.

So, who was Jack of Badsaddle? Was he a local man who killed the last wolf in Northamptonshire, or was he Sir John de Withmayle, who owned land at Badsaddle, or was he the mythical god Odin?

# Walk 13: Silverstone to Abthorpe

## Silverstone – Abthorpe – Silverstone

**Distance:** 8 miles

**Terrain:** Easy

**Starting Point:** Stocks Hill, Silverstone GR 668442

**Map:** OS Pathfinder 1023 Towcester and Silverstone

---

**1.** Begin in the centre of old Silverstone at Stocks Hill, where there is a newsagent and general store. Almost opposite a mellowed stone house with bow windows, turn into Church Street. Just past this dwelling, go left to follow a narrow, hard-surfaced path to the rear of houses and to a little wooden gate with a marker sign.

**2.** Through here, turn right into a field. There is a spread of woodland in the distance. Keep a straight line through several kissing gates to Pyghtle Cottage at West End. Long ago, this was probably a forest ride and the headless ghost of a hunter is said to have been sighted here.

**3.** Turn right then left by Chequers House into Blackmires Lane. The concrete road to Blackmires Farm crosses the fields and by the rim of a wood that is known for its mass of early bluebells and sweet woodruff. Bear right to the farm. This section of the route may become messy in adverse weather conditions.

**4.** Turn right at the bridleway and through an iron gate. Pass a pond where, in summer, swallows dip and dive in search of insects, then continue into Bucknell Wood. Keep on to the next marker, coming to a broad track which angles the path. Look out for the old yew trees growing around the meeting of the ways. When the path bends around to the right, a 'walkers only' sign indicates the narrow way ahead.

**5.** Go through the gate to exit the wood, then over the short field and the next to Abthorpe. Over the low hill, with Hayes Farm two fields away, glance over the shoulder at the pleasing prospect of Bucknell Wood. A gate in the left-hand corner bears a disc and opens to a green lane.

Turn sharp right through another gate. Here appreciate the expanse of rolling countryside as the spire of the church at Abthorpe becomes prominent. Pass through a ridge-and-furrow meadow, making for the short lane to the village.

**6.** Turn sharp right for the route back to Silverstone. The well-trodden path hugs the hedge and takes you over a stile as you leave Abthorpe.

From the disc, cross towards Hayes Farm, with Bucknell Wood to the right. Cross the ditch. Make for the large gate at the edge of the trees and pass to the next field. Skirt the chicken farm to go over a stile between the bungalow and the wood.

**7.** Cross the lane – Challock Farm is directly opposite. Proceed to a further stile and a planked bridge.

In the next field, veer to the right and over the stream to a finger-post for Towcester. After another bridge, join a narrow path by the brook. This leads between garden fences to Little London at Silverstone, and to Stocks Hill.

## Silverstone – The Legend of Whittlebury Forest

Silverstone once lay within the confines of the Royal Forest of Whittlebury. Even today, there are still compartments of the old forest close by, such as Hazelborough Forest and Bucknell Wood. These are now administered by the Forestry Commission. Prior to the reign of Edward I, a royal hunting lodge nestled in the heart of the forestation. It was sited close to a number of fishponds. Earthworks are still evident in the environs of Little London. It is believed that refugees fled from London to live here at the time of the Black Death.

Way back in the mists of time, Whittlebury Forest was the setting

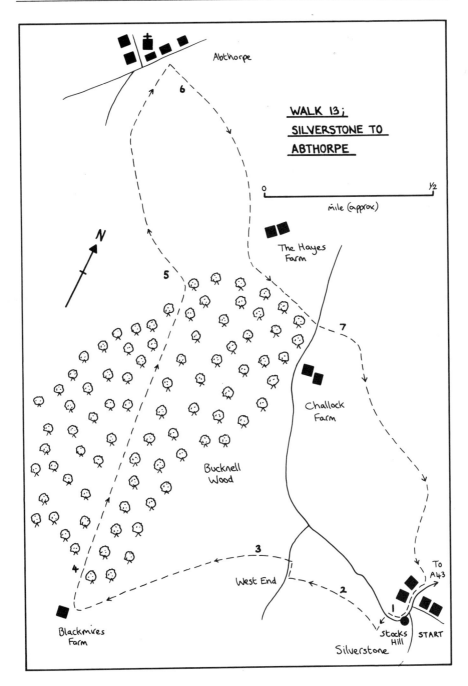

for more than one macabre legend. A noble ranger and his beautiful daughter lived in a cottage on the fringe of the woods. She attracted the attention of a young knight, who fell deeply in love with this ravishing wench. The girl encouraged him with her coquettish airs, but soon she tired of him and spurned his advances with an attitude of coldness and contempt.

The gallant knight, driven to despair by her rejection, committed suicide by decapitating himself with his own sword. Before long retribution was to fall on the ranger's callous daughter. She also died, and was doomed for eternity by the relentless quest of the headless huntsman.

> *'That she, who I so long pursued in vain,*
> *Shall suffer at my hands a lingering pain.*
> *Received to life that she may daily die,*
> *I daily doomed to follow, she to fly.'*

From 'Theodore and Honoria' by John Dryden (1631-1700)

This tale might possibly have been handed down from ancient Germanic folklore, which tells of a supernatural huntsman who haunted the vast forests of Europe, chasing prey to the end of time.

## Whittlebury Forest and the Wild Hunt

In Anglo-Saxon times, tradition has it that the 'Wild Hunt' was both seen and heard in the wide tracts of the forests of Whittlebury and Rockingham. In this county it was known as the 'Wild Men' and the 'Wild Hounds'. Along the shady glades, these 'Wild Men' were reputed to give a loud whoop to encourage their dark, wide-eyed hounds to follow. A chronicle of that era, at Peterborough Abbey, described how 'the spectral hunters ushered in a time of disaster'. The 'Wild Hunt' was alleged to have been sighted in the deer park at Peterborough, also in the woods around Stamford. The monks at the abbey were said to have heard the demonic riders blowing their horns in the darkness.

There could have been aspects of the Germanic God Wodin in the wild huntsman, for he was their God of War. The Anglo-Saxons appear to have honoured him above any other pagan god and gave his name to communities in England. To the Norsemen he was Odin, a tricky god of magic and disguise. It was believed in Britain that before Christianity came to these isles, Wodin led a pack of baying hounds across the stormy winter skies, leaving death and destruction in their wake.

As the God Wodin or Odin gradually faded in people's memory, the Devil took over as leader of the 'Wild Hunt'. According to folklore he was the seeker of lost souls, abetted by his spectral huntsmen and their fearsome hounds.

# Walk 14: Southwick

*Southwick – Crossway Hand Farm – Southwick Wood –*
*Lodge Farm – Southwick*

**Distance:** 5¾ miles

**Terrain:** Moderate

**Starting Point:** The churchyard, Southwick GR 021921

**Map:** OS Pathfinders 918 Peterborough (South) and Wansford TL09/19, and 917 Corby (North) and Uppingham SP89/99

**1.** Start at the corner of the churchyard at Southwick, where there are two bench seats. Turn into the main street. Opposite the church is a most attractive stone house, Church Cottage. A few metres away is the welcome sight of the 17th-century pub, The Shuckburgh Arms, with a thatched roof. Proceed through the village to the lane that leads to Bulwick.

**2.** After 1½ miles on this quiet stretch, watch for the bridleway post on the right which directs to Crossway Hand Farm and Boar's Head Farm. The broad track skirts the edge of Southwick Wood to eventually reach Boar's Head Farm. Stay on the grassy track to the perimeter of the trees and enter the wood through the opening. Head straight on to a disc on a post.

**3.** Turn left and carry on until another track crosses the path. There appears to be no obvious direction at this point.

**4.** In fact, you go right here to follow the path to a waymark by a bridge. Cross here then go straight up the slope, to the left of the hedge. The footpath curves the same way around a dilapidated red brick barn.

Ignore the path ahead to go sharp right at the next marker, alongside a small wood, which may be scattered with celandines in the early

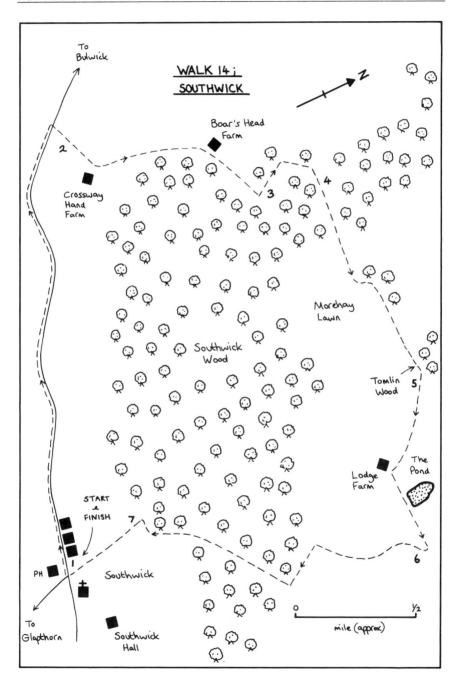

To
Bulwick

**WALK 14;**
**SOUTHWICK**

N

Boar's Head
Farm

2

Crossway
Hand
Farm

3    4

Morehay
Lawn

Southwick
Wood

Tomlin
Wood    5

The
Pond

Lodge
Farm

START
&
FINISH

7

PH

Southwick

6

To
Glapthorn

Southwick
Hall

0                    ½
mile (approx)

part of the year. Look across the open fields to Morehay Lawn where, with field glasses, it is possible to see the remains of the old oak trees known locally as the Druid Oaks. Please do not stray from the right of way for a closer look at the ancient trees as they stand on strictly private land. It was at Morehay Lawn, in the 17th century, that a clash between George Lynn and Sir Mildmay Fane took place, resulting in disaster – see later.

**5.** At the next disc another track angles over the path, but you keep straight on, with the hedge to the right. Go through the farmyard of Lodge Farm. Look for the waymark on the telegraph pole, then go on past The Pond. This small lake is often alive with busy waterfowl.

**6.** Turn off the hard road into a field, following the hedge and ditch on the right alongside a wood. Cross the footbridge into cover and continue to the next marker. Go up the long steep slope then bear left to cross a further track. Your route now runs along the edge of the wood, with landscape in view, and bearing to the right.

**7.** Turn sharp left into fields toward Southwick, glancing over for a glimpse of Southwick Hall and the short spire of the church. Once over the wooden footbridge and the brook, the way passes between stone walls at the side of the churchyard to return to the beginning of the circular walk.

## Southwick Hall and Church

Southwick is a tiny, one-street community situated in glorious walking countryside, with a great swathe of forest brushing the village. A variety of walks start from a single public footpath, which leads from the church. The forest, known as Shire Hill Wood or Southwick Wood, is very ancient and a part of Rockingham Forest, an enormous tract of medieval hunting ground then reserved 'for the monarch's pleasure'.

Southwick Hall is one of the oldest houses in the county, dating back to the 14th century. Throughout its history it has belonged to only three inter-related families, namely, the Knyvetts, Lynns and Caprons. The Knyvetts built the house in 1300, of which the two towers and adjacent rooms remain. John Lynn, who married Joan

Knyvett, bought the hall from his wife's family when they got into financial difficulties. The Lynns owned the house between 1441 and 1840. George Lynn was one of the eight Bannerol-bearers at the funeral of Mary Queen of Scots at Peterborough Cathedral. It is believed that the Queen's burial certificate was walled-up somewhere within Southwick Hall. This family made several architectural additions to the property, yet throughout its history it has retained much of the medieval layout. In 1841 the house was bought by George Capron, whose descendants still own the hall. It is open to the public on certain days during the summer season.

The ancient church of St Mary dates back to 1230. Sir John Knyvett, Lord Chancellor (died 1381) to Edward III, and a member of the family which built the hall, built the tower and spire in 1350. It is well worth looking at an outstanding monument on the north side of the chancel – a memorial to George Lynn, who died in 1758. This distinguished work of art is attributed to the gifted Georgian sculptor, Roubilliac, and thought to be his last work. George Lynn is portrayed on the oval medallion, whilst below is the grieving figure of Ann, his wife. Her husband was a man of wide interests, both antiquarian and scientific. His carefully detailed records of rainfall at Southwick were used in a similar study of East Anglia in recent times.

## Morehay Lawn

Morehay Lawn lies north-west of Southwick. Peter Hill, in his excellent *Rockingham Forest – Then and Now*, gives an insight into the management of the medieval forest. Rockingham Forest was so extensive in the Middle Ages, stretching from Northampton to Stamford in length and from the River Welland to the River Nene in width, that it was divided into three compartments of control, called bailiwicks. These areas of jurisdiction were Rockingham, Brigstock and Cliff (King's Cliffe), each being responsible for its own affairs. These sections also contained land that did not belong to any specific parish and was thought of as extra-parochial.

Morehay Lawn was in the bailiwick of Cliff, where the keeper in charge lived in a lodge within the boundary. The 'hay' in the name signifies an enclosure, usually for the purpose of hunting. Charles I sold many mature trees on this tract and pocketed the proceeds for his personal use! The old oaks that remain are little more than decayed remnants of their former glory, though they still exude a certain magic. Over the centuries, this mystical stand of trees has given rise to superstition and theories concerning Druidical rites.

Known locally as the Druid Oaks, they might have marked the boundary of Morehay Lawn, but they are believed by some to be indicative of a sacred site. The Druids were the priesthood of the pagan Celts and scarce information may be gleaned from an account written by the Romans. The supposedly secret rites were deemed to have taken place in the oak tree groves. The Druids believed the oak and the mistletoe to be sacred and that the latter had medicinal properties, calling the plant 'all-heal'. This parasitic growth had to be gathered from the source at a specific time and in a particular way. It was cut with a golden implement, six days following a new moon and collected in a white cloth so that it didn't touch the ground.

At the time of the Roman invasion of England, dense forests of oak and other native trees, such as ash and hazel, covered most of this county. Perhaps the Druids did, indeed, perform their sacred rituals beneath the majestic boughs of Morehay Lawn.

## The Legend of Morehay Lawn

Lady Lynn and Sir George Lynn lived at Southwick Hall at the end of the 17th century. Lady Lynn believed that her husband no longer loved her and that his feelings towards her were cold. She became flirtatious with a young neighbour of theirs, Mildmay Fane, who lived nearby in a grand mansion at Apethorpe. At Christmas, Lady Lynn had given a ring to Mildmay, in the hope of making George jealous. This, however, failed to work, as her husband agreed that 'the ring was fair'. His wife took this as confirmation that he did not care for her, as he dismissed the incident without further comment.

Little did she realise what a drastic turn of events she had set in motion! Far from being indifferent to his wife's gift to Fane, George Lynn was furious and suspected the couple of conducting an affair. He told her that he was going out hunting with Mildmay Fane before dawn the next morning. The two men met at Morehay Lawn, which lay between their two properties, at early light. What happened next will always be shrouded in mystery. Did the rivals meet in the woods to fight a duel? Or did Fane pretend to mistake Lynn for a deer, whilst all the time planning to murder his mistress's jealous husband? Or maybe it was just a tragic accident?

Whatever the reason, before long George Lynn lay upon the ground writhing in agony from a fatal wound from Fane's pistol. The perpetrator of the act leapt guiltily on to his horse and, without a backward glance at the critically injured man, fled northwards. The dying man lifted his head and said, 'God be praised he rideth north.' This was, in fact, in the opposite direction to Southwick Hall and Lady Lynn.

As Lady Lynn sat at her spinning wheel, she became worried when her husband failed to return by midday. As she mused on the problem, there was a sudden disturbance outside her chamber. 'What is this?' she cried, as four men burst into the room before her servants could stop them. They carried in her husband and placed him on the floor. Lady Lynn threw herself upon his body, begging him to speak to her. 'Oh George, come back to me,' she implored. 'Who can have done this to him? May he be cursed for this deed.'

The villagers could not tell her who had killed her husband. They had searched the ground around the dying man, but did not find a weapon. However, one of them handed her a ring and said, 'We found this, Lady, a ring.'

The widow took the band from him and shrieked in horror, for it was the very ring that she had given to Sir Mildmay Fane. Her plan to bring George back to her had gone hideously awry!

# Walk 15: Charwelton to Fawsley

*Charwelton – Church Charwelton – Fawsley –*
*Charwelton*

**Distance:** 4½ miles

**Terrain:** Some steep slopes, and the waymarks may be confusing.

**Starting Point:** The packhorse bridge, Charwelton GR 566568

**Map:** OS Landranger 152 Northampton and Milton Keynes

**1.** Start at Charwelton, on the Daventry to Banbury road (A361), five miles south-west of Daventry. The medieval packhorse bridge is not far from The Fox and Hounds. A finger-post close by marks the Jurassic Way. There is also a disc with the shell logo, the symbol of this 88-mile long-distance walk from Banbury to Stamford.

Once over the first field and footbridge, there is a brief spell along a narrow lane, over a blue-brick bridge and then over ridge and furrow meadows to Church Charwelton and the site of the deserted village. Here remain signs of the medieval fishponds adjacent to the isolated church of the Holy Trinity. Tufts of lichen cling to the ancient walls and there are cool stone seats beneath the vaulted roof inside. Here there are monument brasses and effigies from the 15th century to members of the wealthy Andrews family, contemporaries of the Knightleys, on the neighbouring estate at Fawsley.

**2.** On leaving the churchyard, step off the Jurassic Way to head for the stony track skirting several barns. Go up to the road and straight over. Continue through two gates then, as you breast the hill, Badby Downs enhances the pastoral scene. Your path falls into the hollow and rises in front of Fawsley Farm.

Turn right into the lane, now at Little Fawsley, to pass the flats, formerly the domain of the Steward of the estate. Walk along the lane to

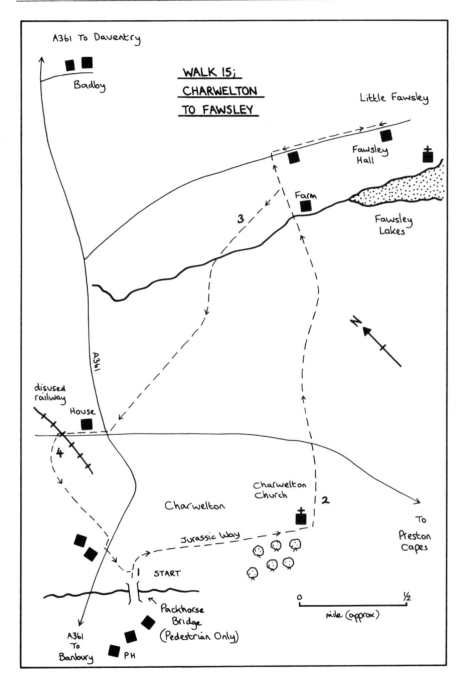

the ponds and the elegant Fawsley Hall Hotel, standing grandly in the park and within sight of St Mary's Church. Turn and retrace your steps to the gateway of Fawsley Farm and the finger-post to Charwelton.

**3.** Just before the farm buildings, pass through the gate on the right, going downhill (toward the distant telecommunications tower) to a small pond. Keep a slanting line to two far gates.

Turn left. There may be a 'temporary diversion order' at this point, though it is a puzzle to know which of the two discs to follow. At certain times heavy crops could be a problem. In general, go down the slope to the crossroads at the A361, on the outskirts of Charwelton and to the sign for Canons Ashby (National Trust).

Enter the opposite road (to Priors Marston) for a short way – just past the iron-sided bridge you get a glimpse of an early ventilation shaft for the dismantled railway.

**4.** Turn left into the field to join the Jurassic Way to the village and to return to the packhorse bridge.

## Murder at Charwelton

Charwelton straddles the main road (A361), close to the neighbouring county of Warwickshire. In medieval times it was a prosperous community with many safe hostelries, but it went into decline when a new village sprang up a mile distant from the church. In the 14th century, a road of sorts linked Daventry and Banbury, and a packhorse bridge over the Cherwell carried the merchants, and travellers and all their baggage. The ancient bridge is still used by pedestrians today, though it is only 1 metre (3ft) wide. It has two pointed arches and a cutwater, and is considered to be a prime example of a medieval bridge.

In the 19th century a notorious murder took place at Cherwell House, a 16th-century farmhouse a short distance from the village, on the Hellidon road. The place was demolished and replaced by a farmhouse in 1978.

The murder of a wealthy farmer, John Clarke, shocked the gentle inhabitants of Charwelton. The deed was committed on the afternoon of Saturday, 10th February 1821, when Mr Clarke was cutting hay from a rick near to his home. There was no warning, but suddenly there was a loud report from a gun being discharged and the farmer collapsed in agony from a massive injury to his left arm. Anthony Marriott, a farm worker, ran to his master's aid and dragged him into his house. He peeled off the man's coat, and Mrs Clarke bound up the shattered arm to staunch the profuse bleeding, urging the labourer to hasten for the doctor.

A surgeon from Daventry, Mr Wildgoose, eventually arrived at the farm and examined the injured man, whose arm and main artery had been brutally damaged by the shot. The surgeon told the farmer that he would have to amputate the limb in order to save his life, whereupon Clarke insisted on making his will before the operation. The executor for the patient, Mr Robert Canning, placed a guard around the barn from which it was thought the gun had been fired, possibly from an aperture beneath the tiles.

The following day Canning ordered men to search the barn, where they discovered a shotgun, a ladder, wallet, bacon and bread, and also a fustian bag containing lead shot buried in the straw. A further foray on Monday revealed a man crouching in the barley stack. The culprit was Philip Hayes, an ex-employee, who was immediately arrested and charged with the wilful shooting and fatal wounding of John Clarke, and consequently committed to the county gaol.

The condition of the victim deteriorated after the futile operation, and on Tuesday, 13th February, he died, at the age of 67 years. He left a younger wife, Mary, who was 35, with their two children. It appeared that she had been having an illicit affair with Philip Hayes for some time. He had been engaged as a farm labourer, and Mary had probably become bored with her elderly husband and fallen in love with Hayes. After only six months in his employment, Clarke had sacked the chap after an argument, but the enamoured couple continued their adulterous relationship. Mary was clearly the instigator of the attempted murder and was obsessed with the idea of getting rid of her husband. Her lover had seemed only too willing to acquiesce to her wishes.

After Hayes was arrested, further evidence was found at his lodgings when letters written to him by Mary Clarke was discovered. In one of them she wrote, 'If it is not done soon I cannot see what will be the end of it. I wish you would do it as soon as you possibly can. It seems strange, that you should be so long about it.'

Mary Clarke was arrested a week after her husband died, and charged with being an accessory to his murder. Together with Philip Hayes, she was sentenced to be executed on Saturday, 10th March 1821. A great crowd gathered at Northampton gaol for the public hanging as the trial had caused a sensation throughout the county.

## Fawsley

The parish of Fawsley supposedly takes its name from the Saxon word for the colour of the grazing fallow deer, at one time so common to the area. Fawsley Hall, a most stately mansion, faces the peaceful parkland, whose extensive grounds were landscaped by Capability Brown. It was the seat of the aristocratic Knightley family for 500 years from the 15th century and it is recorded that Queen Elizabeth was entertained here. The vast park was a deer hunting ground for Charles I when his troops were amassed at Borough Hill, near to Daventry, preceding the Battle of Naseby in 1645.

Georgian and Victorian wings were added to the early Tudor house over the centuries, resulting in the magnificent façade and stunning bay window. The 14th-century ironstone church of St Mary, protected from animals by a ha-ha, bears testimony to the prolific Knightley dynasty in monuments, brasses and heraldic glass. Now standing apart, it once had the company of a settlement, though that has long since vanished.

# Walk 16: Wicken to Puxley

## *Wicken – Puxley – Wicken*

**Distance:** 4 miles

**Terrain:** Easy – no stiles

**Starting Point:** Cross Tree Road, Wicken. GR 745395

**Map:** Landranger 152 Northampton & Milton Keynes

---

**1.** Only a remnant of the trunk of the original Gospel Elm remains in Wicken. A plaque is inscribed, 'Under this elm since 1587 a service to mark the joining of the two parishes has been held every year on Ascension Day.' A similar tablet nearby records a 'new Gospel Elm planted December 1985, donated by Wicken Horticultural Society'.

In Cross Tree Road, admire the beautiful lych-gate to the parish church before setting off.

**2.** Turn left into Church Lane and left again into Whittlebury Road. Go past Pound Close, which takes its name from the stone pound, and veer to the right. The countryside is rather flat but, nevertheless, pleasant, with Wicken Wood complimented by the ever-changing patchwork of hedgerows and fields.

The lychgate to the parish church

Proceed to the sign directing to Deanshanger, Lillingstone Lovell and Whittlebury, near to the Wicken Toy Centre. Note the latter finger for a few metres and go over the stream.

**3.** Turn right at the public footpath to Puxley sign and past the back of a barn, ignoring the road that goes to Folly Field Farm. Proceed until the hedge comes to an end. The path now carries on to a boggy patch and skirts a clump of small trees.

Keeping the hedge to the right, go through a gap to a three-armed post on a broad grass strip (the post indicates the way to Puxley).

**4.** Through the iron gate is the Green Acres Riding Centre, and a second gate opens to Puxley.

**5.** Turn right and follow the lane out of the hamlet to a fork in the road. Take the right side, going along the narrow lane until it bends sharply toward Deanshanger.

Go through the iron gate on the right. Although there is a "Private" sign on the gate, the landowner has left room for the bridleway at the left-hand side of the hedge. Carry on across the next two fields, through two small iron gates, still on the left. Follow the path at the right-hand hedge and proceed until you get to a lane. Cross over where, directly opposite, there is yet another iron gate with a marker sign. Go through this gate and keep straight ahead; on the right, there is a barbed wire fence. The path soon dips down to the brook in the right-hand corner of the field where there is a wooden bridge. Go over the bridge and up the slope, keeping to the left. The path eventually slips between two hedges adjacent to the sports field and into the village.

**6.** Turn left to pass Church Close and Church Green to finish the circular walk.

## Puxley Law

The hamlet of Puxley is neighbour to Deanshanger, a mile north along a narrow lane. Even today Puxley exudes a remote air, and the name itself has a sinister ring. Puxley means 'Goblin's Clearing', a haunted glade in the wood where one might have the misfortune to

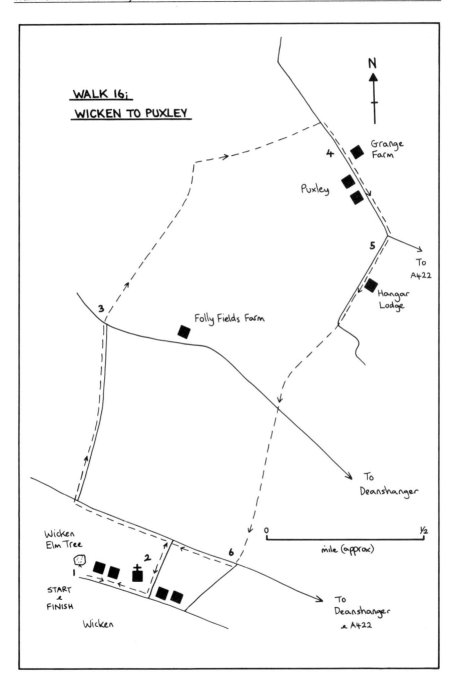

WALK 16;
WICKEN TO PUXLEY

N

Grange
Farm

4

Puxley

5

To
A422

Hangar
Lodge

Folly Fields Farm

3

To
Deanshanger

0                    ½

mile (approx)

Wicken
Elm Tree

2

6

1

START
&
FINISH

To
Deanshanger
& A422

Wicken

meet a grotesque sprite or, even worse, an evil spirit. In medieval English the familiar word 'Puck' was sometimes used to describe the Devil!

Puxley once lay within the limits of Whittlebury Forest, which as late as the 1780s was very dense. The Fox and Hounds, shown on Bryant's map of 1827, was in the vicinity of Hanger Lodge at Puxley, although the ale-house vanished long ago. A strange event took place in The Fox and Hounds in the 19th century. A group of men were gathered at the inn and one of them refused to finish off his drink. His companions could not believe their ears and said that 'a man that refused to drink of his cup should be hanged'.

The drinkers must have been highly inebriated for they decided that John Windmill should be put 'on trial' there and then. A miller from Passenham was declared to be the judge, and others posed as sheriff and the jury. Taking the law into their own hands, unwisely, they hanged poor Windmill with a length of cord. It was only the quick thinking of Janet Thompson that saved him, although she had scant concern for the victim, remarking that 'they were spoiling her cord'.

The miscreants were brought to justice at the High Court and charged with conducting an unlawful and riotous assembly, though what became of the villains is not known. Anyone who refused to finish off his glass was, after this, locally referred to as subject to 'Puxley Law'.

## Wicken

Wicken is a typical Northamptonshire village. It lies close to the border with Buckinghamshire and three miles from Watling Street (A5). Wicken was divided into two parishes in the 15th century, when the stream between the two settlements of Wykedyve and Wykehamon was recognised as the boundary. Each parish had its own church, St John's for the former and St James's for the latter. The present church of St John's replaced an earlier thatched church constructed of cedar wood. The church of St James was lost nearly 250 years ago. In 1587 the twin parishes were reunited and called Wicken. Since then, in every successive year, without a break, this event has been celebrated on Ascension Day.

An old custom of eating spiced caked on the occasion still persists. At the conclusion of the special service, held where the ancient elm used to stand, under the new Gospel Elm, the gathering joins in Psalm 100 then the food is distributed. The old recipe for the spiced cakes may be of interest:

'Three Bushels of Wheat to be made into cakes with six pounds of Butter, six pounds of Currants, a pound of Carroway Seeds with as many cloves and allspice as will make up one shillingsworth in the whole. Sixteen cakes of the largest sort to weigh six pounds of each into the oven. All the remaining Flour to be made into cakes to weigh four pounds and half into the oven.'

# Walk 17: Easton-on-the-Hill

*Easton-on-the-Hill – Wothorpe – Stamford –*
*Easton-on-the-Hill*

**Distance:** 6 miles

**Terrain:** Moderate

**Starting Point:** The signpost at the corner of Park Walk, Easton-on-the-Hill GR 012043

**Map:** OS Explorer 15 Rutland Water and Stamford, and OS Landranger 141 Kettering and Corby

---

**1.** Easton-on-the-Hill is a delightful limestone village two miles south-west of Stamford, on the A43 from Corby. Start at the post to Wothorpe, at the corner of Park Walk, and follow the stony track down the hill, bearing right at the next sign – to Stamford Road.

Carry on down to the plank bridge over the stream and uphill to a stile in the left corner of the field. Cross here, with excellent views of Stamford, and make for the gate onto the main road (A43 Corby to Stamford).

**2.** Turn right and walk for a short distance along the pavement toward Easton-on-the-Hill.

**3.** Cross at the finger-post 'Bridleway to Wothorpe', observing special caution on this busy highway and concealed bend. The hard track bears left, bordered by hawthorn and blackthorn bushes, to pass through the trees, revealing a very pretty walk. Ignore the track joining from the left and keep straight on as the picturesque ruins of Wothorpe Hall come into sight. Use the pedestrian bridge over the Stamford bypass and continue through the spreading chestnut trees to the Old Great North Road.

**4.** Cross and turn left. For about half a mile you will be on the pavement, against the high, stone perimeter wall of Burghley House.

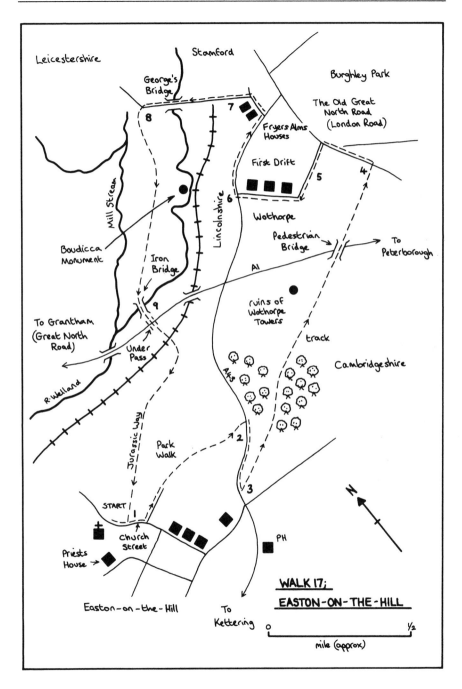

Leicestershire

Stamford

Burghley Park

George's Bridge

The Old Great North Road (London Road)

8

7

Fryers Alms Houses

First Drift

Mill Stream

Lincolnshire

5

4

6

Wothorpe

Boudicca Monument

Pedestrian Bridge

To Peterborough

Iron Bridge

A1

ruins of Wothorpe Towers

To Grantham (Great North Road)

9

track

Cambridgeshire

Under Pass

A43

R. Welland

Jurassic Way

Park Walk

2

3

START

Church Street

PH

Priests House

Easton-on-the-Hill

To Kettering

N

**WALK 17;**
**EASTON-ON-THE-HILL**

0            ½
mile (approx)

**5.** Look for the bridleway sign on the far side of the road, going over to First Drift. Ignore the bridleway on the left. You should follow the road through this residential area.

**6.** Turn right at the end then continue to the A43. Cross the road and turn right towards the town, staying on the pavement past the High School tennis courts and Daniel's football ground.

**7.** Bear left by a row of terraced almshouses (Fryers), go over the railway bridge then down to the River Welland and over by George's Bridge.

**8.** Keeping the river on the left, cut over The Meadows to a gate by the riverbank. Keep on over the grass, which is often ablaze with buttercups in early summer. A plaque states that the Roman ford lies on one of the most important roads to the north, from London to Lincoln. In AD61, Queen Boudicca, whose monument adorns the river's edge, pursued survivors of the 9th Roman League.

**9.** Cross the iron bridge over the water-course of the River Welland, which is clear and alive with fish. Join the Jurassic Way.

Bear left across the field toward the A1 and go through the underpass of the motorway. Use the plank bridge and then approach the railway line. Proceed over the level crossing with great care and vigilance. Turn right over a wooden bridge to climb a very steep hill. Pause to look back at the extensive vista over the ancient town – at least four church towers may be spotted. Look for the narrow concealed gap in the hedge on the right to pass over two fields, coming to the rear of Easton House. Watch for the distinctive Jurassic Way logo and continue into Church Street to complete the circuit.

## Easton-on-the-Hill

Situated 2 miles south-west of Stamford, Easton-on-the-Hill has immense charm. It has a host of handsome dwellings built of local limestone and topped by the famous slate, which was quarried in the immediate vicinity. Many of these are listed buildings and therefore protected. From certain angles on this walk, whatever the season, the subtle overall colours and textures create a pleasing tableau.

Although no longer commercially viable, the quarry area is now a

Nature Reserve and SSSI (Site of Special Scientific Interest), and colonised by a plethora of interesting flora. The pre-Reformation Priest's House, of the late 15th century, though later restored, was initially a rectory and scant in size. Currently viewing of the limited museum is possible. National Trust details are on site.

Lloyds of London, the prominent insurance company, have a tenuous link with this village. Lancelot Skinner, son of a former rector, was on the ship La Lutine when she floundered and sank off the coast of Holland in 1799. The vessel was carrying a cargo of gold insured by Lloyd's. The ship's brass bell was salvaged from the wreck and continues to play a vital role. It is rung to signify a maritime loss, and hence known as the Lutine Bell.

## Wothorpe Towers

The dramatic ruins of Wothorpe Towers are tucked away on the county boundary with Cambridgeshire. It was built for Thomas Cecil, Earl of Exeter (died 1623), the eldest son of Lord Burghley, not far from the family seat at Burghley House at Stamford. It is said to have afforded a handy haven from the upheaval of cleaning of the great house, as well as a reception for visitors!

Wothorpe Towers: the ruins of Wothorpe Hall

---

# Walk 18: Titchmarsh

---

*Titchmarsh – Titchmarsh Nature Reserve – Aldwincle –
Thorpe Waterville*

**Distance:** 6 miles

**Terrain:** Easy

**Starting Point:** The Dog and Partridge, Titchmarsh GR 022798

**Map:** OS Landranger 141 Kettering, Corby.

---

**1.** Start at the Dog and Partridge at the green in the centre of the village. A memorial seat is over the road. Carry on to Church Street and St Mary's Church, noted for the magnificent tower topped by sixteen slender pinnacles. Approach via the unique ha-ha (ditch) forming the boundary wall and note the tiny scratch or mass dial, which might be easily missed, on a buttress close by the porch. Look up to the sundial on the face of the tower.

**2.** Go through the churchyard to leave on the lower side. A little to the left (just off the route), at Islington, is a row of substantial stone dwellings, the Pickering Almshouses. They were built as a hospital in 1756 'for eight poor persons', and endowed by local patronage in 1862 and the following year as an asylum for 'two bedeswomen' and 'two bedesmen'.

**3.** Return to the finger-post in the lane then continue up the slanting, sloping path over the hill, overlooking the wide spread of the Titchmarsh Nature Reserve. Engage extreme care in crossing the A605, where there is sometimes a snack van on the Fishermen's Lay-by.

**4.** Stay by the hedge to meet the Thrapston Town Walk, going right. This was the original line of the railway before it was dismantled some years ago and now forms an integral part of the circular walk

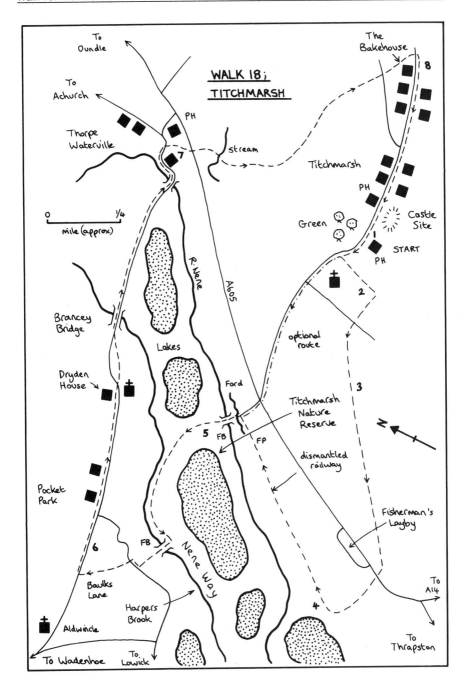

WALK 18;
TITCHMARSH

To
Oundle

To
Achurch

Thorpe
Waterville

PH

stream

7

0    ¼
mile (approx)

R. Nene

A605

Brancey
Bridge

Lakes

Dryden
House

Ford

Pocket
Park

5  FB

FB

6

Baulks
Lane

Harpers
Brook

Aldwincle

To Wadenhoe

To
Lowick

Nene Way

The
Bakehouse

8

Titchmarsh

PH

Castle
Site

Green

START

PH

1

2

optional
route

3

Titchmarsh
Nature
Reserve

dismantled
railway

FP

N

Fisherman's
Layby

4

To
A14

To
Thrapston

around this vast nature reserve. **For the shorter circuit:** it is possible to take a shorter route back to Titchmarsh. Turn right and follow the track which leads back to the A605, opposite to the road which leads back to Titchmarsh. Cross the busy main road carefully and follow the minor road back to the village, as shown on the map.

**5.** Where the path meets the vehicle track, turn over the ford and bubbling spring alongside and cross the river bridge, with Titchmarsh Mill and The Middle Nene Cruising Club in the distance (no public right of way). Follow the waymarks over the narrow stream to the car park at Lowick Road, Aldwinckle. Continue briefly on the Nene Way through the cutting then follow Baulks Lane to Main Street.

**6.** There is another handy seat here for a break before you bear right, past the pocket park, to Thorpe Road. Dryden House on the corner, formerly the old rectory, was the birthplace of John Dryden (1631-1700).

The clear-cut lines of All Saints Church are an eye-catcher, though the church is now redundant and administered by the appropriate trust. On the curve, a short cut takes you over the field, avoiding the nasty bend, then rejoins the road close to Brancey Bridge (from 1760) over Harpers Brook. The raised walkway, a relic of earlier flooding on this stretch, conveniently affords the walker a grand-stand view of the lakes.

The road soon bumps over the River Nene and The Staunch before Thorpe Waterville. At the T-junction, step back to observe the singular sight of a countenance on the facing end of a grand barn (it is clearer in winter when the trees are bare). This is the lingering remnant of an edifice, a fortified manor back in 1301, next to Thorpe Castle House.

**7.** Over the stone slab stile, a short path winds around to the A605, which must again be traversed with caution (fast moving traffic). Drop down the bank beside the brook to field level.

At the sturdy bridge, take a diagonal line, rising on a modest gradient to Titchmarsh. There is a superb view of the church on the horizon – a landmark on most of this walk. This spot was the obvious choice for a beacon site, one of many in our county, in the anxious era of the anticipated invasion of the Spanish Armada in 1588. The path goes to the extreme left of the village, to a quiet lane with a few modern homes.

**8.** Cross here to pass through the hedgerow and outskirts and to filter into the lower end of High Street beside the Old Bakehouse. Turn uphill on the raised pavement to pass the ancient castle site, bus stop and the Wheatsheaf Inn on your return to the start.

## Aldwinckle

The charming village of Aldwinckle probably derives its name from the Saxon word 'wincel' for a bend or corner. It is situated above the River Nene, making a great double bend between Wadenhoe and Thorpe Waterville. The wide main street has fine stone houses and, unusually, a parish church at either end, as the community was once divided into two parishes. They were ultimately united in 1879.

In the 17th century two prominent men were born here, and if that were not coincidence enough, each was born in one of the rectories. Thomas Fuller was born in 1608 in the rectory of St Peter, where his father was rector. The house was demolished in 1790. Thomas Fuller became curate of St Benet's in Cambridge whilst a very young man. He was a staunch Royalist and Chaplain to the King's forces. Fuller was an important writer on religious works and a notable Church of England historian. One of his most famous works was *Worthies of England* (1661), which contained references to Northamptonshire, including 'an apple without a core or rind to be pared away'. He died in 1661 at the age of 53 years.

The church of St Peter dates back to the 12th century and is reputed to have one of the most elegant broach spires in the county.

John Dryden, also a prolific writer, was born in 1631 in the room over the front door of the rectory of All Saints. The building is now known as Dryden Cottage and is on the corner opposite the church where his grandfather was rector. John Dryden was the eldest child of Erasmus Dryden, whose parents came from Canons Ashby, and Mary Pickering of Aldwinckle. Their son was a poet, playwright,

critic and supporter of Oliver Cromwell. After James II came to the
throne, Dryden became a Catholic and wrote his famous but contro-
versial poem 'The Hind and the Panther'. As a result of his adher-
ence to his new faith he lost his position of Poet Laureate, to which
he had been appointed in 1670, but continued as a very productive
writer to the end of his days. He died in May 1700, and was given an
impressive funeral at Westminster Abbey, where a hundred car-
riages took part in the procession.

The church of All Saints has a magnificent 15th-century tower
with one bell, but the interior is from the 13th century and has a
600-year-old font. The church is now administered by the Redundant Churches Commission.

## Titchmarsh

Titchmarsh stands high on a ridge overlooking the wide green valley
of the River Nene. The glorious 15th-century perpendicular tower of
St Mary's Church, an impressive landmark, rises to 99ft and may be
seen by the traveller from the main A605 road between Thrapston
and Oundle. It is said to be the finest church tower outside
Somerset. The churchyard has the unusual feature of a ha-ha as the
boundary on the west and south sides.

In the High Street (opposite the pub), over a wall, lies the site of
an early medieval castle, though only a vague outline of mounds and
ditches is visible. In the 13th century Maud de Sisenham became the
sole heir to her father's Titchmarsh estate. As a Ward of the King she
was given in marriage to Sir John Lovell of Minster Lovell in
Oxfordshire, who was a powerful man in the Court of Henry III. After his marriage to Maud, the Manor House at Titchmarsh became
the Lovell's principal seat. In 1304, Maud's son John, obtained a
licence to fortify his house into a castle-like residence. Four generations of the family lived there, each male heir being named John, but
by 1364 the place was in a ruinous state.

## The Mistletoe Bough

The following events are supposed to have taken place at
Titchmarsh Castle at the wedding of Sir John Lovell and his bride.
The grand wedding feast took place in the great hall, gaily decorated

with laurel and holly branches. Green bunches of glistening mistletoe berries hung from the oak beams and the yule log cast flickering shadows on the stone walls. The bridal pair and their favoured guests were seated on the dais at the head of the hall. Two long tables were set down on each side of the room and crowded with servants and villagers. Their merry shouts and laughter almost blotted out the music flowing from the musicians who played in the gallery. After the feast and the dancing were over, the young bride, her eyes alight with excitement, suggested a game of hide and seek. She was only 17 years of age and looked very pretty in her long gown of silk, with a jewelled circlet on her tresses.

Before anyone could stop her, she jumped up and ran out of the hall, calling over her shoulder, 'Lovell, be sure to be the first to find my hiding place.' She sped down a long, cold corridor until she reached a small, arched doorway. Pushing the door open, she discovered a spiral stone staircase. The girl climbed the steps, up and up, until she came to a tiny round room at the top of the tower, where there was a solid oak chest. She heaved and tugged on the heavy lid until it came open, and climbed in. There was plenty of room for her slight frame, and she made herself as comfortable as possible. The massive lid closed on top of her with an ominous bang, for little did she know that the iron catch to secure it could only be opened from the outside.

The bridegroom and all the company searched all that night, the following day and then many more, but all in vain, she was not to be found, it seemed. Much later, when most of the guests had long since passed away, a skeleton was discovered in an old oak chest. The secret hiding place was revealed at last! The bones were draped in a tattered and faded silk gown, with a jewelled circlet around the skull. Why no-one had thought of looking in the big oak chest remains a mystery. The tale of the missing bride is told in an 1830s ballad called 'The Mistletoe Bough' by T.H. Bayley and Sir Henry Bishop. The song was to become popular in Victorian drawing rooms.

# Walk 19: Ashby St Ledgers

*Ashby St Ledgers – Welton – Grand Union Canal –*
*Ashby St Ledgers*

**Distance:** 7 miles

**Terrain:** Initially hilly, then towpath with easy surface

**Starting Point:** The church, Ashby St Ledgers GR 573681

**Map:** OS Landranger 152 Northampton and Milton Keynes

**1.** Start at the church of Ashby St Ledgers, adjacent to the striking Manor House. Look through the gate-piers to the timbered Tudor gatehouse. (The long-distance footpath, the Jurassic Way, a part of the return route of this walk, passes down the lane to Crick, where the posts are etched with the fossil shell Kallirhynchia sharpi, resembling a scallop on the waymark disc.)

**2.** Walk forward and left at the T-junction on the Welton road. As it curves and splits, see the wooden post and stile. Proceed toward the horizon as the path dips and rises several times over the limestone hills prior to Welton.

**3.** Turn briefly left into the village street then pass down Round Close and go left at the bottom, opposite The White Horse, signed Well Lane.

Cross near the phone box to the huge chestnut tree and a post to Norton on a shaded, sloping path. Cross the Daventry road. Take a slanting line over the pasture to an extremely high stile and a bridge with a chain, just clipping the corner of the next field as you continue to a small gate. Go forward on the bridleway to the concrete ramp, bridge and hedged-in path (which may be muddy) then up the slope to the GUC (Grand Union Canal) brick bridge.

**4.** Drop down left to the towpath and under bridge number 8 to a

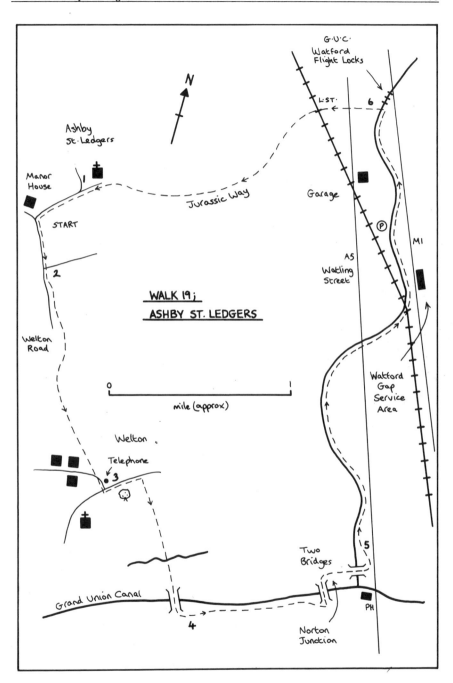

N

G·U·C·
Watford
Flight Locks

Ashby
St·Ledgers

L·ST·

6

Manor
House

1

Garage

Jurassic Way

P

M1

START

2

A5
Watling
Street

WALK 19;
ASHBY ST. LEDGERS

Welton
Road

Watford
Gap
Service
Area

0

mile (approx)

Welton

Telephone

3

Two
Bridges

5

Grand Union Canal

PH

4

Norton
Junction

slight blip, then go down the steps or over the hump to bridge number 10 and a milepost to Braunston.

The Northampton Branch of the Inland Waterways Association, with the assistance of British Waterways, has undertaken a scheme of replacement of the missing cast-iron mileposts on these banks. Thomas Milner, the GUC Company's northern district engineer, measured the entire length of the waterway with a steel tape, completing the mammoth task in 1893. He reversed the earlier trend by starting from Braunston.

At the meeting of the slightly oleaginous, lazy waters at Norton Junction, note the smart, informative signpost which declares 'Leicester 41¼ miles, Brentford 89¼ miles, and Braunston 4¼ miles'.

A short diversion to The New Inn (on the A5) at Buckby Lock may be taken at this point by remaining on the towpath. The flight of seven locks has a 19.2-metre fall.

**5.** Otherwise, go up and over bridge number 10 and the white wooden bridge. In this serene setting, carry on ahead as the towpath meanders along on a high bank and the landscape drops away beyond the hedgerow. As the subtle curves of the canal unfold, the walker will appreciate the changing vistas. Once past Welton Hythe Marina, the growing hum of traffic of the motorway disturbs the tranquillity, but fortunately, only temporarily.

The brightly painted railway bridge has classical motifs, arches and ribbed brickwork, and the path brushes the brash perimeter of Watford Gap Service Station. The Stag's Head displays an inviting frontage. Slightly ahead, a shallow weir must be negotiated (except, of course, in flood conditions). Mercifully, the intrusive sounds of man fade and tranquillity is soon restored. A black iron plate (number 21) on the bank reads 'Living Milestone'. This is not far from the winding-pool, where boats may turn around to avoid the Watford Flight of seven locks and a rise of 16 metres. It is very pleasant to just watch the fascinating activity at this point, with the constant flow of boats either going up the flight or down, in the agreeable setting around the Lock Keeper's Cottage.

**6.** The route now departs from the waterway, so at the second lock turn over the little footbridge, leaving the jurisdiction of British Waterways.

Go down the slope and over the fence and a low-lying rough patch next to the Toll House Garage. One is then jolted back to the rude awakening of the A5. A finger-post on the grass verge displays the decorative logo of the Jurassic Way, which is now followed to Ashby St Ledgers. Cross here with extreme vigilance, then shortly approach, within a bowshot (or so!), the unavoidable hazard of the high ladder-stile (not suited to those less able) on either side of the railway embankment (though it is well marked). Easy terrain now stretches ahead on the final mile to Ashby St Ledgers and leads directly back to the church.

## Welton Folklore

Welton graces a hilltop and takes its name from the many springs in the vicinity. Its location is enhanced by the views over the valley and the sinuous lines of the Grand Union Canal. A strange tale is told of a bewitched family who lived here in 1658. Widow Stiff had two daughters; the younger was ten years old, the age of her sister unknown.

It began with the younger girl, who suddenly started to vomit water, sometimes as much as three gallons (14 litres), much to the bemused attention of the onlookers who had crowded into the house to witness the strange goings-on. The child went on to regurgitate a vast quantity of dry items, such as coal and stones, some so large, weighing 4 ounces (115 grams), that she could hardly eject them from her mouth! This continued for two weeks, and while it lasted other queer things began to happen. Articles of furniture started to move about of their own accord. Bedclothes sprang off the bed, as if yanked by an unseen hand. Flax would not burn on the fire, and every time a door was shut to one room, a sack of wheat would not remain upright, but toppled over. Things in the hall would spin about when the occupants of the house were not looking. An invisible force spilled milk, and a mischievous spirit threw about pellets of bread. Many other tricks were played, some amusing, some not.

A few people who had long been suspected of witchcraft were arrested and one of these sent to gaol. It was said that the woman persisted with her pranks in the prison, but Widow Stiff was much reassured when the woman was sentenced, for it seemed to have a quieting effect on her girl and her household. Although it was thought that the daughter of the widow was bewitched, it would seem to be a case of a poltergeist. This phenomenon is often associated with an adolescent child, more often that not, a female. Poltergeist activity appears to be some form of excess energy, not yet understood. The surfeit of this force usually manifests itself in a young person, when all sorts of irritating and meaningless activities transpire. An outbreak of poltergeist eruption is sudden, with mysterious bangs and crashes. Heavy furniture may be shifted about and small objects fall from mid-air. Disturbances may last for a few days or even weeks. Eventually, as in Widow Stiff's Welton household, the upheaval declines and the family return to their normal, peaceful existence.

Sally Davis

# Ashby St Ledger

The church of the Blessed Virgin Mary and St Leodegarius, in the parish of Ashby St Ledger is the keeper of important brass memorials. These are accessible, though hidden from immediate view. One of these is of William Catesby, a former Chancellor of the Exchequer and Speaker of the House of Commons. He was beheaded in 1485 after capture at the Battle of Bosworth, where Richard III was slain.

The Catholic Robert Catesby, five generations later, was heavily fined for his faith and was forced to sell his property in Oxfordshire and became domiciled with his mother at Ashby. His bitterness gave rise to his involvement with the Gunpowder Plot, whose aim it was to blast the Houses of Parliament to smithereens. It is reputed that secret rendezvous were held in what is now known as the Plot House, or the timbered gatehouse.

When Guy Fawkes was apprehended in the cellars of the seat of government on November 5th 1605, along with the damning evidence of the gunpowder barrels, Catesby and his fellow conspirators galloped away from London, to escape into the forested countryside. They were eventually caught at Holbeach in Staffordshire, where Catesby and Thomas Percy were finally killed by a single bullet which pierced both bodies as they defiantly stood back to back! Other irreplaceable relics and treasures lie within these ancient walls and do note the handsome ogee arch doorway in the porch.

# Walk 20: Fotheringhay

*Fotheringhay – Elton – Yarwell – Wansford – Nassington – Fotheringhay*

**Distance:** 12 miles (but easily shortened as there are several easy linking ways at each village)

**Terrain:** easy, flat country near to the Fens

**Starting Point:** St Mary's and All Saints Church, Fotheringhay GR 060932

**Map:** OS 152 Peterborough and OS Pathfinder 918 Peterborough and Wansford (South) TL09/19

**1.** Start at Fotheringhay, at the T-junction at the gates of the most elegant church of St Mary and All Saints, facing the Nassington road. Go forward over the first bridge and Willow Brook to a finger-post pointing to Elton (at the time of walking a temporary order closure was in place).

**2.** Otherwise, continue on the road to the top of the rise, where there is a finger-post on both sides. Turn beside the ash and oak trees to follow the track over the dismantled rail line towards the distant river and lock. Elton church tower can be seen among the treetops.

**3.** A smart timber bridge spans the River Nene for village access. Next are Elton Lock and the derelict mill of 1840. A mighty chestnut tree graces Stocks Green, and the mellow houses and Crown Inn create a pleasing ambience – as do the names bestowed by proud residents, such as Waddle End. There is a tantalising glimpse of Bury Leas behind the wall.

**4.** Leave on the path besides the Nassington road to cross at the byway sign to the dirt road. Ignore the left curve and in a few metres a disc will direct you through a poplar plantation to an iron bridge.

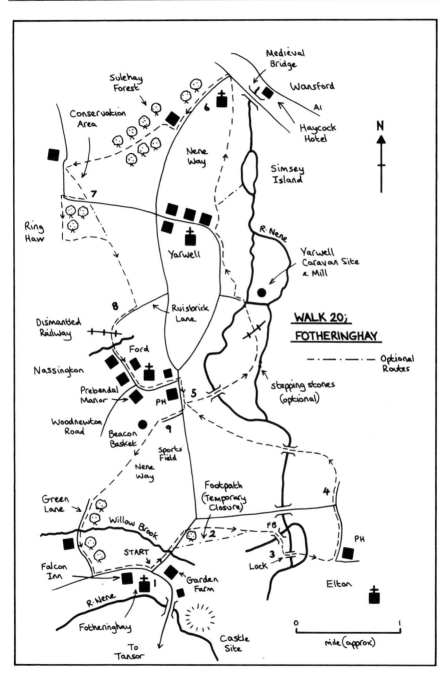

Medieval Bridge
Wansford
Haycock Hotel
A1
Sulehay Forest
Conservation Area
Nene Way
Simsey Island
6
N
Ring Haw
7
R. Nene
Yarwell
Yarwell Caravan Site & Mill
Ruisbrick Lane
**WALK 20;**
**FOTHERINGHAY**
Dismantled Railway
8
Ford
Nassington
Prebendal Manor
PH
5
stepping stones (optional)
— · — · — Optional Routes
Woodnewton Road
Beacon Basket
9
Sports Field
Nene Way
Green Lane
Footpath (Temporary Closure)
4
Willow Brook
START
2
FB
PH
Falcon Inn
3
Lock
Elton
R. Nene
1
Garden Farm
Fotheringhay
To Tansor
Castle Site
0                    1
mile (approx)

The path now takes an oblique angle over several fields as the spire of Nassington Church beckons.

**5.** Stay on the grass verge for a few metres only, without going into the village, as the circuit now joins the Nene Way over the meadows. For the agile and adventurous, there is a challenging set of stepping-stones midstream (optional).

Carry on to Yarwell Mill and Caravan Site, just skimming the edge, and quickly cutting through to the main street. The way is well signed to Wansford. Note Simsey Island, a lozenge-shaped strip in the middle of the river, perhaps taking a brief diversion to take a closer look.

**6.** At Wansford, on the long, arched bridge, go left and uphill (or right for the Haycock Inn). Skirt the church as you proceed into Yarwell Road to commence the return leg of the walk. Stay beside the woodland and the sign for Wansford Pasture, The Wildlife Trust nature reserve, notable for its wetland.

Just after Forest Lodge there is a finger post and hand gate into Old Sulehay Forest. The shady path through the old wood eventually opens to a gate blocked by an enormous stone slab, opposite the entrance to the 17th-century Sulehay Lodge.

**7.** Nature lovers will appreciate an easy, open track through the Conservation Area. It offers an opportunity to enjoy the colonised slopes of the former quarry on the way to the Yarwell road.

Although the post opposite directs a similar line, this may be difficult to follow and it may be simpler to backtrack on this road to the bend and take the byway on the outlined circular walk.

Following on from the forest exit, turn left and continue to the byway, passing Ring Haw. Look for an offset finger-post to Yarwell by the rubble of a fallen wall. Stay to the right of the hedge then go through gaps in the next two fields. If you tried the short cut, it rejoins here.

**8.** Go sharp right over and down the slope, to ultimately merge into the uneven surface of Ruisbrick Lane, bordering the defunct clay pits. Pass beneath the old railway bridge and through the shallow ford, to enter the outskirts of Nassington.

Veer left at the triangle to Church Street. The Three Horseshoes, the historic Prebendal Manor, All Saints Church, the Weslyan Chapel of 1872, the village hall and the school are set between charming houses and intriguing barn conversions edging the wide road.

**9.** Round the bend at the Black Horse, the path soon peters out at a stony lane and Nene Way sign (opposite the outward path to Yarwell). The sports field is at the end, with a commemorative 'beacon basket' on the far side.

Round the deserted building, go straight down and through the hedge to follow the well-posted route up the hill to the rim of a spinney, where the Way makes a slight dog-leg to the right and stays close to the trees. A bridleway allows the path to filter in, passing Walcot Lodge and cottages, then bearing left to meet the Woodnewton road out to Fotheringhay. Return to the gates of the church.

Sally Davis

## Fotheringhay Castle

There almost seems to be a curse on specific environs, as though their occupants are constantly prone to misfortune. In medieval times such a venue was Fotheringhay Castle, in this superb setting with the River Nene flowing serenely by the foot of the hill.

When Simon de Liz espied the place, he recognised the potential and consequently built the castle on the mound. Upon his demise, his widow married David, King of Scotland, and subsequently the property passed down through the Scottish dynasty to John Le Scot, Earl of Huntingdon, who was to die bereft of an heir. Fotheringhay Castle rapidly descended through a number of families until it reverted to the Crown in 1296.

In retrospect, an eerie fact emerged: several of the inheritors suffered the death sentence. Throughout its tedious history, it was the base of evil fortune, a gloomy prison and a scene of violent death. No wonder it gained such a macabre reputation! Nowhere else in Britain, apart from the capital, seems to have had the dubious distinction of this ancient pile, where so many Royal personages met an untimely end. The succession of events culminated with the execution of Mary Queen of Scots in the Banqueting Hall of the castle in 1587.

Although Mary of Valence, the Countess of Pembroke, was unconnected with royalty, she appears to have been the first woman to live there whose life was touched by tragedy. Her husband, the Earl of Pembroke, was tragically killed in a tournament on their wedding day. Edward III rebuilt the castle and gave it to his son Edward, Duke of York, who was slain at Agincourt and buried, according to his wishes, in the collegiate church of Fotheringhay.

The next owner of the castle was Richard Plantagenet, Earl of Cambridge, who was beheaded. The castle passed to his son, Richard, Duke of York, who perished in the Battle of Wakefield, together with his second son, Edmond, and both were buried in the church. Richard's widow, Cecile, spent a greater part of thirty-five years of widowhood at Fotheringhay, where her eleventh child, Richard III, was born. She died in 1495 and was buried close to her husband in the church of St Mary and All Saints.

Catherine of Argon received the castle as part of her dowry from

Henry VIII, who had it repaired at enormous expense. When he wanted, later, to make it her prison home, she declared emphatically 'that she would not go unless bound with cart ropes and carried thither'. The Queen chose to go to Kimbolton Castle as a grim alternative.

After James I came to the throne, he bestowed the castle upon three of his courtiers. Following the King's death in 1623, Mountjoy, Earl of Newport, did for the castle what James had never contemplated in the wake of the violent death of his mother, Mary Queen of Scots, the Earl pulled the castle down and disposed of much of the material. The strange jinx was even transferred to the construction of Conington Castle in Huntingdon, where the demolished stone was utilised. The owner of the new castle, Sir Robert Bruce Cotton, died upon completion of this fine residence.

The lovely riverside village of Fotheringhay has reverted to a peaceful existence today, with few reminders of the ill-starred castle, except for the mound and a rough block of stonework from the keep. However, the elegant 15th-century church survives with its octagonal lantern tower, which is a handsome landmark in the otherwise flat landscape. This splendid edifice was once part of a collegiate church established in 1411 by Edward, second Duke of York. Dudley, Duke of Northumberland, on receiving the place as a gift from Edward VI, ordered the demolition of the choir and college buildings. One might even hear the mysterious and plaintive strains of medieval music said to emanate from the lofty interior!

Just to visit the forlorn castle mound and, in summer, see the Scottish thistles that are known as 'Queen Mary's tears' will conjure up the turbulent history of the times.

## Drunken Barnaby

An amusing occurrence concerning a drunken pedlar is said to have taken place in the reign of George III, at Wansford, in the Soke of Peterborough – and so considered to be in Northamptonshire before the boundary changes.

It was on a hot day in July, and Barnaby was feeling very sleepy due to the heat, but perhaps more to the fact that he had imbibed too much strong ale at the tavern. He wandered down the dusty lane until he came to a field by the river, where he espied a comfortable, enticing haycock. Without more ado, he lay down on the sweet-smelling grasses and fell asleep in no time. The sun went behind a cloud and a summer storm blew up. It rained heavily for a short spell, but the slumbering man slept on in a drunken stupor. The river rose over its banks in a flash flood and swept Barnaby away, haycock and all, downstream towards Wisbech.

He awoke startled, feeling lost and alone, and then floated past an excited bunch of people on the banks of the river. He bellowed, 'Where am I?' They yelled back, 'Wansford.' Bewildered, Barnaby questioned, 'Wansford in England?' He thought that he had been swept many miles away, even perhaps down to the sea. Since this handed-down tale persists over the years, the village has frequently been referred to as 'Wansford in England!'

This story appeared in an 18th-century publication *Journal of Drunken Barnaby*. Barnaby is portrayed as a drunken sot as it describes his journeys around England and his visits to Northamptonshire.

There is also a more serious side to the pedlar's frightening experience of being washed down the raging river. From time immemorial, the Nene, which flows through the heart of this county, was known as the rogue river. It was liable to sudden floods after heavy rain, and it was only after the introduction of The Nene Catchment Board in 1930 that the problem was controlled and reduced, though unfortunately it has been known to recur.

Wansford is situated on the banks of the River Nene, where the narrow, arched bridge that used to carry all the traffic on the Great North Road spans the river. The old coaching inn, The Haycock, whose inn sign depicts the story of Barnaby, still carries on the traditional role of catering for travellers.

# Walk 21: Geddington

## *Geddington – Brigstock – Stanion – Geddington*

**Distance:** 8 miles

**Terrain:** Easy

**Starting Point:** Eleanor Cross, Geddington GR 896830

**Map:** OS Pathfinder 938 Corby 88/98

The Queen Eleanor cross

**1.** Geddington is an ancient village, laced with historical interest and intrigue, 2 miles north of Kettering on the A43 to Corby. Start by the exquisite centrepiece of the Queen Eleanor Cross against the backdrop of the church of St Mary Magdalene. The cross was erected after 1294.

**2.** Follow the wall of the school into Wood Street and up the hill to join a rough, metalled road. The sign points towards Geddington Chase and indicates that it is unsuitable for motors.

**3.** Turn right by the farm sheds to follow the byway to Brigstock. Initially, this is a broad gravel path through the wood, which emerges into the countryside. Clay Dick Track runs between growth interspersed with tall ash and oak trees. On past The Chase the blackthorn hedges are strewn with wild sweet peas, speedwell and dog roses, becoming prolific in early summer.

Ignore the footpath into the wood to take the right-hand path, keeping to the edge of the trees as the track dwindles to narrow grass. Carry on past Chase Farm and out on to the metalled Dust Hill Road. Soon, the high, gaunt building known locally as The Matchbox comes into the scene. This prominent landmark was originally built as a clothing factory in 1874 and owned by Wallis and Linnell. Although it was closed down in the 1970s, it has since been revamped in the interior and has retained its business status in another direction.

**4.** Make for the stile and finger-post, to cross into the playing field.

**5.** Left again to head for a stile in the far hedge, bearing right to Harper's Brook and a line of tall trees. Pass into the next field.

Look for the waymark on a post at the edge of the stream and turn away from the water to cross the middle of the field. Remnants of the ancient Rockingham Forest are all around and the sight of the spire of St Peter's Church at Stanion is partially obscured. At the far end, go through a gap in the hedge and straight over, skirting the left hedge, to a reverse disc on the gate. In the middle of the field, search out a marker on the fence and then the next, as the village of Stanion unfolds ahead.

Over the stile, turn right and carry on to the stone-built Mill House, with the busy Brigstock road in the distance. After the wooden bridge spanning the brook, bear left toward Stanion.

Turn right to yet another bridge, which may be almost hidden beneath sloe and hawthorn bushes when in full foliage. Proceed up the bank to the rear of the village hall.

**6.** Continue over the playing fields, past the hall and left into Willow Lane. Just short of the end, veer left into a farm lane.

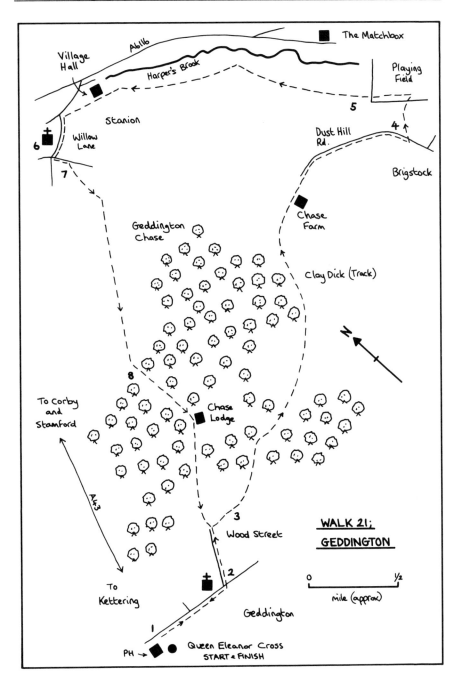

The Matchbox

Village Hall

A6116

Harper's Brook

Playing Field

Stanion

5

Willow Lane

6

Dust Hill Rd.

4

7

Brigstock

Geddington Chase

Chase Farm

Clay Dick (Track)

N

8

To Corby and Stamford

Chase Lodge

A43

3

Wood Street

WALK 21;
GEDDINGTON

To Kettering

2

Geddington

0                    ½
mile (approx)

1

PH →

Queen Eleanor Cross
START & FINISH

**7.** Over the stile, bear right across the field, keeping to the left hedge. At the stile, bear slightly across the field toward a low fence and marker sign. Climb over into the next field and keep to the left hedge. In the following field, continue to an old gatepost and cross a track at right angles.

**8.** You are now entering Geddington Chase, just another lingering compartment of the forest. Seek a marker on the fringe of the woodland. Go forward on the broad grass ride to Chase Lodge, which is set in the clearing.

Pass round the stone house to the right, to make for a similar wide ride in front and more waymarks. Turn away to leave the wood behind. Head for the farm buildings and stile beside a corrugated iron shed. Cover a rough patch of grass to a sign 'Footpath to Stanion' (indicating the reverse route). Complete the circuit back to Geddington.

## Geddington Chase

Geddington Chase is one of the few remaining ancient woodlands and was once a part of Rockingham Forest, understood to be the largest royal forest in England. In the reign of Edward I, the woods stretched from Northampton to Stamford, being 33 miles long and 8 miles wide. Geddington was always a favourite place for the Plantagenet kings (The Devil's Brood), who would frequent their summer palace and hunt the plentiful red deer and boar in the enveloping forest. It is also believed that gunpowder was used for the first time in this country at the royal hunting lodge, in the reign of Henry III.

Although Sherwood Forest has always had first claim to Robin Hood, in the opinion of some local historians, the tale of the daring outlaw originated in Northamptonshire. A man named Robin Hood was held prisoner at Rockingham Castle in 1354, where he awaited trial for 'Trespasses of vert and venison in Rockingham Forest'.

In Burl Bellamy's well-researched book *Geddington Chase, the history of*, he mentions that during the middle of the 16th century, the Crown yielded very little profit and that, in fact, commoners gained more than the monarchy. As a result of inadequate administration, squatters made their homes in the forest wastes and the secluded villages became the haunts of vagabonds and robbers. This was especially true of Brigstock and Stanion, which were notorious enclaves for deer poachers, even with the threat of execution if proved guilty.

Geddington Woods became a hiding place for stolen cattle, horses and goods. There might even be treasure buried in the Chase, as Thomas Clerk and Thomas Lea broke into Wingfield House in Derbyshire, where Mary Queen of Scots was being held, in 1576, stealing money and jewellery. They made their escape southward to Rockingham Forest, but were captured and taken to Leicester Gaol, then on to London. Whilst in captivity, they confessed to hiding their loot in Geddington Woods. It was decided that the thieves should be returned there to try to recover the stolen goods, but the outcome of the search is not known and remains an elusive mystery.

Many of the woods in Rockingham Forest were divided, deforested and sold into private hands, but Geddington Woods survived into the 17th century with most of its boundaries intact. James I was very fond of hunting and killed a large, fat buck here in 1616. By 1676 the Montagu family at Boughton House owned the woodland and the Crown severed its ties with this ancient tract of forest, later to become Geddington Chase.

## Geddington

Geddington has long been a centre of attention and remains so, particularly by virtue of its royal connections and the highly acclaimed Eleanor Cross, the focal point of the community. A 'medieval medley' might describe this important residence of our early rulers. A succession of kings and queens and their various entourages frequented the hunting lodge to the north-east of the church, in the vast reaches of Rockingham Forest. These tracts were exclusively reserved 'for the monarch's pleasure', at a time when the illegal killing of a deer brought about the ultimate penalty of death.

The factual, romantic story regarding the handsome Eleanor Cross is, in itself, a reflection of the Middle Ages. Eleanor of Castile, beloved wife of Edward I, died, in Harby, Nottingham on 28th November 1290, as they went with their army to fight the Scots. Her mourning husband accompanied the funeral cortège back down south to London for her burial at Westminster Abbey.

Four years later, Edward ordered a monument, a cross, to be erected at each place where her procession had halted overnight. Her body had rested in the church of St Mary Magdalene, which is of Saxon origin, and the adjacent memorial declares this fact. In all, twelve crosses were commissioned, another in this county is at Hardingstone, though the one at Geddington is acknowledged as the finest surviving dedication to the queen. Charing Cross, in the capital, is a replica of the first, which was destroyed.

It is recorded that William of Ireland, evidently a worthy mason, was paid the sum of £3 6s 8d for each statue he carved of the queen, which must have been a grand award in those remote times. A canopy protects each of the three figures, although, sadly, the faces are showing signs of deterioration. At the foot of the steps is concealed Roman well. Stroll along to the heavily restored 13th-century bridge, which probably carried the poignant procession over the River Ise. The cutwaters and pointed arches are still evident, but the structure now has restricted traffic access.

## Geddington Chase: A Ghost Story

Pat lived in a keeper's lodge in the 1970s, with her husband and three young daughters. Carol, the baby of the family, was a good deal younger than her two sisters were. When the child was only three years old, her mother went up to Carol's small bedroom, where she slept on her own. Expecting her to be fast asleep, she was astonished to hear her talking, then she giggled as though someone was tickling her, and sang loudly. Pat went into the room and found the child sitting up in bed waving her arms about, and thoroughly enjoying herself, as if she had a playmate! Her mother went downstairs after settling her daughter for the night, and laughed about the incident with her husband. They decided that Carol had acquired an imaginary friend, as very young children are prone to do.

However, one night Pat was coming out of her own bedroom

when she saw an unsteady light coming up the stairs. Thinking it was one of her older daughters playing with a torch, she called out to ask what she was doing. At that moment, a slight and unknown figure materialised on the landing. A young woman, clothed in a long black dress and wearing a white cap, was carrying a flickering candle. The woman appeared to be highly anxious and peered into all the rooms as though seeking someone or something before fading away.

Carol continued to talk and sing with her imaginary friend every night before she went to sleep. Gradually she started to call him by name: Peter. She sometimes said that his sister, Georgina, came to join them. There was nobody of that name in the family and Pat did not recall ever repeating it to the child, and it was a rather difficult name for a little one to pronounce. These nightly visits by Carol's friends went on at intervals for three years. The strange thing was that, unlike most imaginary pals, their presence did not exist outside the bedroom. Most children carry on talking and playing with their unseen companions in daylight, even occasionally insisting that an extra place be set at the table, but not Carol. Peter and Georgina only came to life in that little bedroom at night.

One day Pat was talking to an old man who had lived in the village all his life and was a great one for local stories. She mentioned the ghostly young woman she had encountered in the house, and he was not surprised. He knew all about the house being haunted. His version of the tale was that many years ago, there had been a fire in that house and the two children and their nursery maid had perished in the blaze!

## The Giant Dun Cow of Stanion

Reposing in the graceful old church of St Peter at Stanion there is a very strange relic measuring almost 2 metres (6ft) in length. According to local legend it is a massive rib of a giant dun cow.

An enormous animal wandered into the village one day, and no one knew whence she came. All efforts to trace her owner failed and the good people of Stanion decided to adopt the quiet and docile cow. The inhabitants treated her well, and even found a large barn to shelter her over the cold winter and a milkmaid, called Mary, to attend to her welfare. The dun cow became the communal beast and rewarded the peasants by providing them with rich, frothy milk. No matter how large the vessel placed beneath her, she would fill it without fail.

It was well known in the area that one did not venture out to Burton Wold on certain nights of the year. It was a meeting place for a coven of witches, and on moonlit nights they performed their weird rituals and danced on the Wold. One of these witches, who came from Brigstock, vowed to play a spiteful trick on the innocent people of Stanion. Hiding a sieve under her cloak, she crept along to the cow one morning, long before the milkmaid had risen, and placed the riddle under the giant cow. Valiantly the poor animal strained to fill it, but, of course, the precious milk ran away through the holes and the cow died from utter exhaustion.

The villagers were heartbroken over the loss of their bovine benefactor, and buried it in a field to be called 'Cowthick', but not before taking a rib from her lifeless body and placing it in the church, as a reminder of their beloved Dun Cow. They thought that the wretched witch would not dare to exercise her evil powers in the sacred building. The bone has been here in safekeeping for centuries and people have imprinted their initials all over the surface.

However, some folk do not believe this tale to be true and say that the bone is from a whale and brought back long ago by a traveller in foreign parts. What is the origin of this baffling relic? Who put it there and why? It is a puzzle that will probably never be solved!

# Walk 22: Salcey to Piddington

*Salcey Forest – Piddington – Salcey Forest*

**Distance:** 5 miles

**Terrain:** Easy walk – no stiles

**Starting Point:** Car park off the minor Quinton to Hanslope road GR 793517

**Map:** OS Landranger 152 Northampton

---

**1.** Use the Visitors Car Park just off the Quinton to Hanslope road, which runs parallel to the Ml motorway. Salcey Forest is free to walkers, and an adequate map of the forest trails is included in the small charge made for parking. Follow the Great Spotted Woodpecker Trail (red trail) from here, as far as the bridleway. The beginning of the walk is identical to another forest trail indicated by black markers.

**2.** Bear right at the bridleway and Mid-Shires Way, leaving both coloured signs. In the clearing, lady's smock and bluebells carpet the ground early in the year. At the point where another path crosses, carry on. There are markers at regular intervals.

**3.** Turn right alongside the woodland edge, leaving the forest behind, yet staying on the Mid-Shires Way.

**4.** Go left and then through a gap in the hedge into a green lane. High hawthorn hedges closing in might result in a muddy, rutted track in wet weather. The green lane continues over a hump-backed bridge spanning the dismantled railway line, to Church Farm.

**5.** Heed the finger-post which points to the left across the farmyard and into the field. The stubby church tower at Piddington becomes visible.

**6.** Turn right at the next marker, departing the Mid-Shires Way, now on a public footpath. Keep the hedge to the left. Piddington village is off on the other side.

**7.** At the next disc, turn right across the field and stile to the site of the excavated Roman villa. Consistent digging has been in progress here for a number of years.

**8.** Turn left to keep the hedge on the right. At the next disc, carry on past the rear of a timber-built house, and out into the lane at Old End.

The church of St John the Baptist is close by. It was constructed of ironstone in 1280. The inside is as neat and tidy as the churchyard.

**9.** To complete the circuit, turn into Church Road then Forest Road, which leads back to Church Farm.

**10.** Retrace your footsteps to Salcey Forest. Enter the wood and turn right along the horse trail. Re-connect to the Mid-Shires Way and bridleway, as indicated, then proceed to the car park.

Sally Davis

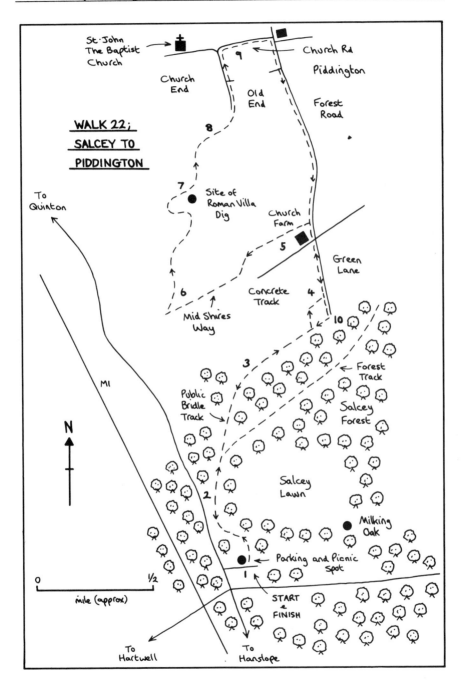

St·John
The Baptist → ✝
Church

Church Rd
Piddington

Church
End

Old
End

Forest
Road

**WALK 22;**
**SALCEY TO**
**PIDDINGTON**

To
Quinton

7

Site of
Roman Villa
Dig

8

9

Church
Farm

5

Green
Lane

6

Mid Shires
Way

Concrete
Track

4

10

3

Forest
Track

M1

Public
Bridle
Track ←

Salcey
Forest

N

Salcey
Lawn

2

Milking
Oak

0                    ½

mile (approx)

Parking and Picnic
Spot

1

START
&
FINISH

To
Hartwell

To
Hanslope

# Salcey Forest

Salcey Forest, which graces the front cover of this book, is a famous oak wood lying six miles from Northampton, on the border with Buckinghamshire. It was the smallest of the ancient royal forests in the county and dates back to Norman times. It remains a compact area of woodland of some 520 hectares (1300 acres), being 2 miles wide and 1½ miles long, from north to south. It encircles Salcey Lawn, a space of 100 hectares (250 acres) now in private hands, which was once grazing land for deer. They numbered around one thousand and roamed the forest freely before the enclosure of 1825. In earlier centuries, any commoner owning land in the parishes adjoining the forest had a right to graze his cattle on the Lawn in the summer months. That is, as many beasts as he could keep on his own land in the winter.

The forest is celebrated for its fine oaks, and the Salcey Oak was probably the largest and best known of the species. This giant once stood at Hartwell, a village on the western edge of the forest. It was thought to be a thousand years old. Though ultimately hollow, its two sound sides formed an archway where, in the early 1800s, ten people could sit in comfort inside the ruined trunk! The girth was 15 metres (47ft) and it was 11 metres (33ft) high. The locals called it Tom Keeper's stable as the man kept his horse there!

Four miles away from this Goliath of trees grew another sentinel, the Church Path Oak. William Henry, 6th Duke of Grafton, inherited vast tracts of land in the south of the county in 1863, and used to rest under its branches on his way to and from the church at Piddington. Sadly, the Church Path Oak fell down at Christmas time in 1995.

Another tree of distinction worth mentioning is the Milking Oak, with a girth in excess of 6 metres (20ft). It took its name from the fact that its wide spread gave shelter from the sun and rain when the milking was done out of doors. This specimen still stands today, about 100 metres from Salcey Lawn. This is one of only four trees to be marked on the Ordnance Survey Landranger maps series.

Yet another named tree is the Piddington Oak. Both of these trees are thought to be over 600 years old and still produce viable acorns. There are ten veteran oaks left within this popular forest, now a favourite venue for walkers and nature lovers alike.

## Piddington Romano-British Villa

Imagine an Iron Age settlement near to where the modern village of Piddington now stands, just a few years before the Roman invasion of AD 43. Probably the farming community was situated near to a great oak forest, with a stream running nearby, and a wide track out of the settlement. There would have been a few round houses encircled by a palisade and ditch to keep the wolves out. The small, square fields would have been planted with crops of barley, wheat and beans. Other fields were kept for their cattle, sheep and horses. These Iron Age folk were also fond of hunting the wild boar that roamed the forest.

The inhabitants of the community lived in family groups in houses thatched with straw, and upright timber posts supported the roofs. The walls were made of wattle and daub. In the centre of the house was an open fire on a hearth. The women cooked the meals on the open fire in cauldrons. At night, the families slept on beaten clay floors, wrapped in animal skins.

Although most of us think of the Iron Age people as having a rather primitive lifestyle, they were, in fact, a very advanced civilisation. They wove very good woollen cloth and made fine pottery fired in bonfire kilns. But it was their ability to work in metal that really distinguished them. They were brilliant craftsmen in metal, and made swords, farming tools and jewellery. These late Iron Age folk were also very artistic and decorated much of what they made.

Although they were a proud people and were good fighters, able to defend their homes against most attackers, they were no match for the well-organised Roman army. The Romans conquered Britain but the way of life for the inhabitants of Piddington changed very little and changed very slowly.

The small community at Piddington continued to flourish and grow after the Roman invasion. By the end of the first century AD, a stone villa was already under way on the site of the earlier native settlement. It developed into a wealthy and pretentious winged, corridor building, with a bathhouse, garden and a large mosaic floor in at least one room. Unfortunately, some misfortune or disaster overcame the villa and by the 4th century this sophisticated dwelling had deteriorated into a series of squalid hovels for a few families living within the ruins of the villa. However, they were still able to obtain fine pottery.

Since 1979, Piddington has been the setting for a long-term excavation of a known, but almost forgotten Romano-British building, by the Upper Nene Archaeological Society. Perhaps the most significant find was the discovery of a series of 2nd-century stamped tiles, which almost certainly were made on the site. The tiles were stamped 'TCY' and 'TIB CL, SEVERI' respectively, 'SE' appears to have been added to the latter stamp.

There is a strong indication that Roman citizenship was given to a minor British chief at the time of the conquest, perhaps in return for smoothing the way for the Romans. He appears to have taken the name of the Emperor Claudius so his first two names were Tiberius Claudius. We do not know his Iron Age third name. Later, the family took the names of further Emperors such as Verus and Severus. It is truly amazing to have this unique record of two successive owners of a villa estate in Roman Britain and dating from the first century AD.

The Society hopes to carry on working at the site for some years yet and there are exciting plans to open a museum to be set up in a redundant Wesleyan chapel at Piddington, which the Society has purchased, to display and interpret the material from the villa.

This information about the Iron Age and Roman site at Piddington has been kindly provided by Roy Friendship-Taylor, Chairman of the Upper Nene Archaeological Society, and his wife, Liz Friendship-Taylor.

# Walk 23: Oundle to Cotterstock

## *Oundle – Cotterstock – Oundle*

**Distance:** 4 miles

**Terrain:** Easy, pleasant walking

**Starting Point:** Oundle Town Hall GR 033880

**Map:** OS Landranger 141 Kettering and Corby

---

**1.** Oundle Town Hall was built in the Tudor style in 1826. It stands aloof in the Market Place, where the A427 runs through the hub of this distinguished town, to link with the A605 to Peterborough at the bypass roundabout on the outskirts. Leaving the centre, cross the narrow, light-controlled North Street and go on past the football ground.

**2.** At the garage, turn into New Road, where it might be preferable to avoid the rough track at Occupation Road. Instead, use the stile then run parallel for one field only, rejoining at the sports site.

The path retains a fairly straight course over the playing field, rising slightly beside an old cattle trough, almost lost in the tangles of the hedgerow. Cross several simple bridges to Cotterstock, whose roof-tops may soon be seen ahead. At a lower level, unseen but heard, the River Nene lies beyond the heavy belt of trees.

**3.** In the High Street, turn right past the hall, which is shielded by mature chestnut trees. Go down to the fork in the road, one branches off in front of the Manor House to the church of St Andrew, opposite a Regency house with a charming iron veranda.

**4.** Our eventual route is down the other fork. Just around the corner, at the bottom of the hill, is the converted mill house, sluice and bridge. Adjacent to these is a finger-post to Oundle, directing you on the reverse leg of the circuit.

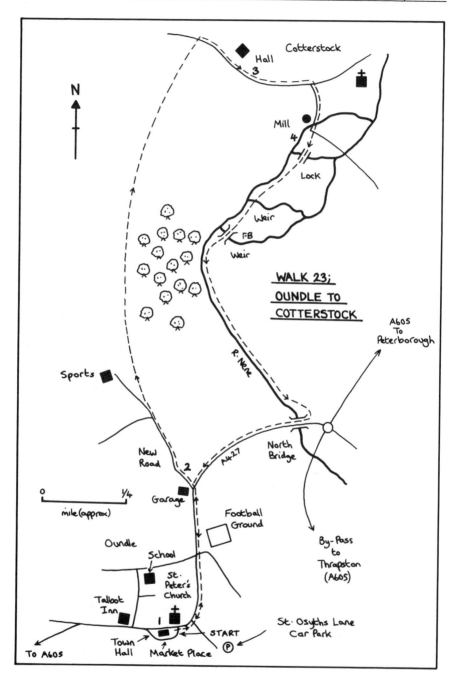

N

WALK 23;
OUNDLE TO
COTTERSTOCK

Cotterstock

Hall
3

Mill
4

Lock

Weir

FB

Weir

R. Nene

A605
To
Peterborough

Sports

New
Road
2

0        1/4
mile (approx)

Garage

North
Bridge

A427

Football
Ground

By-Pass
to
Thrapston
(A605)

Oundle

School

St.
Peter's
Church

Talbot
Inn

START
P

St. Osyths Lane
Car Park

To A605

Town
Hall

Market Place

Go over the lock and weirs as the waters meet, then keep to the winding riverside path to North Bridge and back to the town.

## Oundle

Allow time to explore this splendid, old, stone-built town, where the market bell is still to be heard at midday on Thursday, clinging to tradition, to remind folk of their right to hold a weekly market. The Talbot Inn, dated 1626, is in New Street and not directly on the route of this walk, but it has its own history and haunting. The oak staircase which, tradition has it, was removed from Fotheringhay Castle. The phantom form of Mary Queen of Scots is said to drift down the dark stairs, on her final doomed descent to her execution in the Banqueting Hall at the castle on 8 February 1587.

Close by the hostelry is Drummingwell Lane, though now, sadly, the well is defunct, obliterated by later building. Unaccountable drumming was said to emanate from the well, and perceived to be a dire portent of national disaster. There is an abundance of historically important and interesting places throughout the town, and it might be rewarding to amble amid the more illustrious of these, such as the respected Oundle School, founded by Sir William Laxton in 1556. The major part of this establishment is in New Street, although these hallowed halls are scattered in a number of locations. Please note that the connecting alleyways allow no right-of-way (except the churchyard), but collectively exhibit a unique facet of this renowned seat of learning.

St Peter's Church is celebrated for the exquisite needle-like, octagonal spire dated 1634. Soaring above all, it is a landmark visible from town and country. Jericho, a cul-de-sac tucked away near to the Market Place, is another fascinating find, whose name has been constant for several hundred years. A stone on the parapet of North Bridge records the collapse of the arches in the flood of 1570. It was rebuilt of 'lyme and stonne' the following year.

## Cotterstock

On one of his frequent visits to his cousin at the hall, John Dryden, the county poet, wrote his piece 'Fables'.

Lord Cardigan of Deene had a private wharf constructed here in 1729, when the river became navigable to the sea, allowing development of a commercial trading port.

St Andrew's Church has a Norman doorway and figure above. The 15th-century south porch has a handsome vaulted roof. The church is noted for the fine chancel. It overlooks the river and meadows and was allied to the foundation of a college in 1338.

## Witchcraft at Cotterstock

The unspoilt village of Cotterstock stands above the River Nene. In the early 18th century this remote and undisturbed place was shocked by a bizarre case of witchcraft. Ellinor Shaw was born there and left to fend for herself at the age of fourteen, for her family was poor and could afford no education. Ellinor had a friend, Mary Phillips, who was born in the nearby town of Oundle. For a time they earned their living by honest means, but by the age of twenty-one, Ellinor had become a very lewd young woman. She had become so notorious a figure that when she as much as stepped outside her door, the children would shout after her, 'There goes Nell the strumpet.' These insults only served to fuel her already bitter temperament and she swore she would wreak vengeance on all her enemies.

The two women were said to have devised a plan, to quote an old tract 'they resolved to go to the Devil together'. They were accused of the death by witchcraft of Elizabeth Gorman of Glapthorn, a four-year-old child, along with others in the region. Two constables from Oundle, William Boss & John Soutwell, were witnesses against the prisoners and had them in their charge. They threatened the women with death if they did not confess to witchcraft, and promised their release if they complied. It is no wonder that the poor deluded females concocted such a weird tale of a midnight visitor.

According to their confession, a tall black man appeared before them at 12 o'clock on 12th February 1704. He took Ellinor Shaw by the hand and told her not to be frightened, as if they pawned their souls to him for a year and two months, he would assist them to attain their hearts' desire. The women pricked their fingertips and the visitor wrote a covenant in their blood, which they both duly signed. In fact, this ridiculous tale had the opposite effect, and brought about their downfall and the death penalty.

The two friends were said to have practised evil on others both before and after their confinement. The keeper of the gaol had threatened to put them in irons, and, as a result, was forced to dance naked in the yard for an hour, much to the amazement of the inmates. No one dared to cross the fiendish women, in case they, too, were bewitched. This disturbing behaviour caused the authorities to bring forward the day of their execution, and so, on Saturday, 17th March 1705, the two were brought to the north side of Northampton. The condemned pair were asked if they would say their prayers, but they both laughed loudly and called upon the Devil to help them.

In view of such shocking behaviour, the Sheriff ordered them to be executed with expediency. They were hanged until almost dead and then straw and faggots were lit and they were burned to ashes. This macabre public destruction was watched by a great number of fascinated townspeople.

Witchcraft ceased to be a capital offence in 1736, although the inhabitants of Northamptonshire persisted in their belief in witches long after any other English county, except for Huntingdonshire.

# Walk 24: Braybrooke

*Braybrooke – Brampton Valley Way – Arthingworth –
Braybrooke*

**Distance:** 7 miles

**Terrain:** Moderate

**Starting Point:** Braybrooke Church GR 765846

**Map:** OS Landranger 141 Kettering and OS Pathfinder 937 Market
Harborough SP68/78

**1.** Start from Braybrooke Church in Newland Street and turn away
from the village. Proceed to where the road soon peters out to become an unpaved track. Follow the post indicating the Jurassic Way
until another post shows the public footpath, pointing to the right.

A well-defined footpath goes across the middle of the field, and at
the far end crosses the wooden bridge over the stream to continue
over two fields. Market Harborough now comes into sight, where the
countryside is rather flat. A further bridge and field abuts the
Brampton Valley Way, once a busy rural rail line between
Northampton and Market Harborough. It was operated by the London and North Western Railway, but closed in 1986.

**2.** Climb the ladder-stile on to the Way and turn left, passing an attractive red-brick barn off to the right and under the bridge. The hard
surface path on the Brampton Valley Way is now a fourteen-mile
recreational linear walk between the two main towns. The square
tower of Great Oxendon Church is now visible. The Reverend John
Morton, who wrote *The Natural History of Northamptonshire* in
1712, is buried here.

A stream runs across the path near to a hand gate on the side of the
Way. This is easy walking in a pleasant, tree-lined natural corridor.

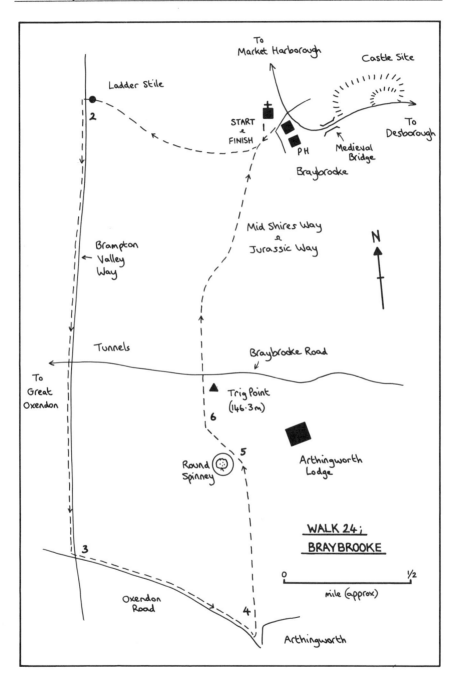

To Market Harborough

Castle Site

Ladder Stile

To Desborough

START & FINISH

PH

Medieval Bridge

Braybrooke

N

Mid Shires Way & Jurassic Way

Brampton Valley Way

Tunnels

Braybrooke Road

To Great Oxendon

Trig Point (146·3m)

6

Round Spinney

5

Arthingworth Lodge

WALK 24; BRAYBROOKE

3

0                    ½

mile (approx)

Oxendon Road

4

Arthingworth

Under the next bridge is the approach to the Oxendon Tunnel, 418 metres long, where a flashlight is recommended to lighten the gloomy conditions. On emergence from the tunnel, the footpath is parallel to the busy Northampton to Market Harborough road (A508). On the banks lining the path there may be a mass of white violets in the springtime.

**3.** Past Station Cottages a gate crosses the track. To leave the line, go through the hand gate to follow the pointer to Arthingworth, 1¼ miles ahead. Another gate gives access to a single-track metalled road, a section of Oxendon road, but unused by traffic.

**4.** At Arthingworth, turn sharp left at the finger-post, on to a short concrete stretch edged by a few houses. After the marker sign, keep to the left-hand hedge of the field. Cross the ditch by a plank, still keeping to the left hedgerow.

**5.** After the next ditch, turn right, keeping the hedge on the same side. Head for Round Spinney, up the hill. Make for the gap in the corner of the field and look for the disc at the base of a tree. There are

excellent panoramic views over the rolling countryside at this point.

**6.** Bear left at the next hedgerow to veer slightly left, in line for the Trig Point indicating 146.3 metres above sea level. Cross over the narrow Braybrooke Road and directly opposite is an unpaved section of Oxendon Road again.

The track follows the right-hand hedge as the spire of All Saints at Braybrooke rises above all. Take a moment to rest on the bench, which has a plaque inscribed 'Braybrooke Parish Council 1995'. Down the hill towards the village, look over the valley of the tiny River Jordan before proceeding to the starting point.

# Braybrooke

Most people who enjoy walking will look at an Ordnance Survey map and be intrigued by the strange names of a locality, and especially by the site of a lost or deserted village, or the earthworks of a long-vanished castle. What did it look like, who lived there and what sort of events took place within these walls?

More often than not, these so-called castles were little more than fortified manor houses that disappeared so long ago that only sparse records survive, except perhaps, when the lord of the manor gave his surname to the nearby community. There is such a castle site at Braybrooke. Fortunately, there are a good number of material sources of the families who inhabited the stronghold. In *Brayborooke, its Castle, Manor and Lords*, written by W. Paley Baildon, F.S.A., and printed in 1923 for a private collection, we are given a detailed account of the residents over hundreds of years and their fascinating genealogy.

Three miles from Market Harborough, on the Leicestershire border in the north-west of the county, the village consists of predominantly brick-built houses, situated in a modest valley. The River Jordan, a tributary of the River Welland, flows beneath the 15th-century bridge in the main street.

The church of All Saints has a slender Perpendicular tower dating back to the 13th century, although most of the surviving structure is from the 14th and 15th centuries. The massive edifice is crammed with interesting features, but the oldest piece in the church is the Norman font, decorated on an aquatic theme, representing intertwining snakes, shells worked into a geometric design and a fish-eating mermaid. In the Griffin Chapel there is an important Elizabethan monument erected to the memory of Sir Thomas Griffin, who died in 1566, and his father who expired in 1609. Close by, in repose, is a very rare wooden effigy of a cross-legged knight, with a shield on his left arm, sensitively carved from a single log of knotty oak. It is the form of Sir Thomas Latymer, the castle builder, who perished in 1333.

The strangest artefact in the chapel is the medallion of a larger-than-life head of a military man, who wears a wreath on his head and three chains around his neck. It was built into a wall of the rectory at Brampton Ash in the 19th century, and placed in the church at Braybrooke in 1933. It is believed locally to have been the keystone from the main keep and entrance of Braybrooke Castle. A protected niche in the wall is the sombre setting for a skilfully fashioned helmet, hammered from a single piece of iron.

## Braybrooke Castle

Sir Thomas Latymer, whose unique effigy lies under the lofty beams, was born in 1270. When he was 23 years old, he obtained a licence to crenellate his manor house, which was to become the early castle at Braybrooke. There has always been a strong conviction in the village that the castle was accidentally blown up, and consequently demolished.

Old records suggest a large and sophisticated manor house, probably constructed of stone, with a great hall and chapel. The roof of the great chamber was of timber taken from the abbey woods at Pipewell, a few miles distant. The buildings stood on a square, double-ditched platform surrounded by a stone wall, with several bridges and gatehouses spanning the ditches. The Latymer family continued to live at the castle until 1411, when Edward died without issue. His sister Elizabeth, who married Sir Thomas Griffin of Gumley, inherited the estate. It was through this lady that her grandson, John Griffin, inherited the castle and the baronetcy. Further information discloses that the Latymers of Braybrooke Castle had a younger son who left to live in Warwickshire. His daughter, Alys, married a yeoman of Snitterfield, near to Stratford-upon-Avon, to become the grandmother of William Shakespeare.

In the 16th century, Sir Thomas Griffin and his wife Jane had three sons and a daughter. The eldest son, Rice, died in 1549. The second son, John, had no children, and the youngest, Thomas, was a lunatic, whose nephew, Edward Griffin, became heir to his estates. Sir Thomas had made a provision in his will for 'his youngest son and daughter Anne to be well looked after during their lives according to their vocation'. Unfortunately, his son Thomas had no control over his affairs, as he had been insane since the age of 12. His father also left instructions to his executors that repairs to the castle were of the highest priority. At that time the hall and chapel were still standing, but had become dilapidated. The executors were to pay for the repairs and the upkeep of the castle during the lifetime of the insane Thomas, at the expense of Sir Thomas Griffin's property. The trust was also to provide sufficient money for the brother and sister to entertain their family and friends, as Thomas was still living in the castle in 1569.

The young Thomas had no offspring, and consequently the property passed to his niece, Mary Markham, and then to the heirs of his uncle, Sir Edward Griffin of Dingley. The last person to live at the castle was probably Elizabeth, the wife of Sir Thomas Griffin, grandson of Sir Edward. This lady is recorded as living at Braybrooke in 1620, after the death of her husband. Sir Latymer's walls were taken down and most of the stone was incorporated into other buildings. It is quite likely that gunpowder was in force to demolish the curtain wall, so perhaps there is a kernel of truth in the belief that the castle was blown up. This is thought to have taken place around 1632, as in a document of 1752 it is stated that the place had been razed to the ground some 120 years previously.

A small manor house was built on the site soon after the action took place, which was to stand until 1959. The manor house or farmhouse, with its mullioned windows, had been deserted for most of this century. All that now remains is the old farm brew-house and the earthworks of the ancient pile of the Latymers.

# Walk 25: Woodford

*Woodford – Denford – Ringstead – Woodford*

**Distance:** 5 miles

**Terrain:** A pleasant, easy circuit

**Starting Point:** Woodford village green GR 967769

**Map:** OS Pathfinder Kettering SP87/97

**1.** Start the walk from Woodford village green, opposite the Duke's Arms, where there is a local information board and ample room for parking, though always with consideration please. Staying on the same side as the pub, walk down past the White Horse Inn to turn left into Church Street. Continue to the dead end then go through the hand gate. Warren Field slopes down towards the water. Further on is the convergence with the Nene Way, parallel to the weir and Woodford Lock. Cross the track of the old railway line and go on to Denford.

**2.** Cross the three bridges on the outskirts of Denford. (You have now left the Nene Way to continue its journey to Islip.) One of these bridges is over the siphonic weir, a device that controls the flow of water from adjacent outlets to ensure the level of water in the navigable River Nene.

Entering Denford through the gate into Meadow Lane, turn right into the High Street. The Cock public house, originally of 1593, is on the far side. In Church Lane, stroll through the churchyard of the church of the Holy Trinity and a delightful scattering of dwellings. Next walk up School Lane and the short, steep hill to the main road. Turn right at the corner. There is no footpath on this unprotected bend, so cover these few metres with caution.

**3.** Look for the set back gateway and the post directing you to

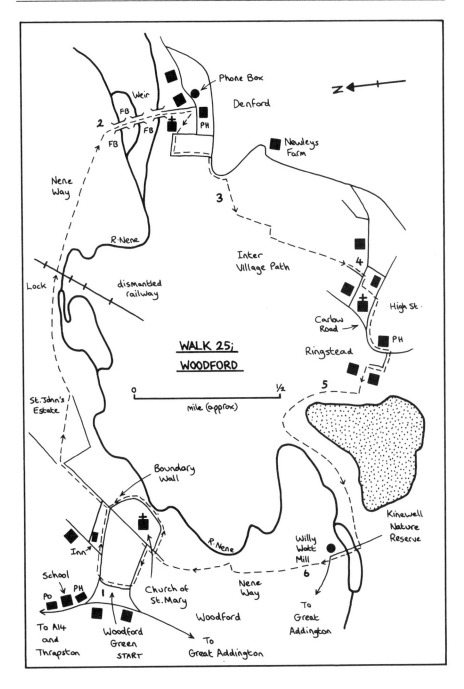

Phone Box
Denford
Weir
FB
FB
2
FB
PH
Nene
Way
Newleys
Farm
R. Nene
3
Inter
Village
Path
Lock
dismantled
railway
4
High St.
Carlow
Road
Ringstead
PH

**WALK 25;**
**WOODFORD**

0                    ½
mile (approx)

5

St. John's
Estate

Kinewell
Nature
Reserve

Boundary
Wall

Willy
Watt
Mill

Inn

R. Nene

Nene
Way

6

School
PO    PH

To A14
and
Thrapston

Woodford
Green
START

Church of
St. Mary

Woodford

To
Great
Addington

To
Great
Addington

Ringstead. A board, sponsored by the Countryside Commission and others, explains the course of conservation of the surrounding landscape. Follow the stony track above the spread of the flat valley for a little way then veer left, with Newleys Farm on the skyline.

**4.** Over the hill, the inter-village path drops down between the houses at Ringstead. On the street, go right to the lane then as far as a stone outbuilding and between the posts to emerge beside the Baptist and Methodist Shared church. Turn right into High Street then follow Carlow Road to the Axe and Compass. Cross the road to walk through Meadow Close and over the brick paving to a private road and an entrance to Kinewell Lake Pocket Park.

A team of diligent conservationists has transformed this quiet nature reserve of 32 hectares (80 acres) from a vast gravel pit, one of a string of workings in the valley. Renowned for its opportunities for nature-lovers of all kinds, it offers an oasis of tranquillity, so kindly observe the few requests regarding litter and sensible dog control to avoid disturbing the wildlife.

**5.** Keep to the path around the lake as it winds along to come close to the river and Willy Watt or Woodford Mill. Go up on to the bridge to look over to the lock, which is often a hive of activity.

**6.** There is a small car park above the roadside buildings and a stile set high on the bank. Joining the Nene Way again, observe the discs to Woodford. The church, standing above the river, soon comes into view.

If there is time it is well worth obtaining the key to have a look round this famous church. (You never know – you might even see the ghost.) Then make a detour round to the back of the churchyard into a very short lane that leads to the old school, now a private residence. Note the heavy wooden door adorned with a large horseshoe that is set into a section of the old boundary wall of the St John's estate. Through here Lady Louisa and other members of the family walked to their place of worship.

Afterwards turn left at the end of the road into Church Street and go up the steep hill of Church Green to return to the start of the walk.

# Woodford

Woodford is a large rural village near to Thrapston, with a fascinating ancient church set on the banks of the River Nene. The parish church of St Mary the Virgin, built in the 13th century, has many secrets and relics, including two rare effigies carved in oak. There are only four known pairs of wooden effigies of couples in England. These two represent Sir Walter Traillys, who died in 1290, and his wife Eleanor, who died in 1316.

The slim figures lie side by side, he wears a helmet and sword and is cross-legged (depicting a crusader knight) and she is shown in a hooded gown. In the last century, naughty children were made to sit on top of the figures if they had misbehaved during the service. The effigies then lay on the floor near to the vestry. The Reverend Smythe had the precious artefacts removed to their present position in the 1850s.

The church revealed one of its secrets in 1867, when a beam was removed in the nave during restoration. An embalmed human heart wrapped in a coarse cloth was discovered. The same gentleman placed this macabre relic in a recess behind glass, in a lofty column where it remains to this day. Why it was hidden from view for so many centuries is a mystery, and no one knows for certain to whom the heart belonged. However, an ancient document kept at Boughton House, near to Kettering, the stately home of the Dukes of Buccleuch, mentions that a Roger de Kirton, a relative of the Traillys family, died whilst on a visit to Norfolk. His heart was brought back to Woodford and lodged in the church in 1260, as was the custom of that period.

Woodford Church revealed yet another of its secrets in 1995, when a time capsule was found during an examination of a beam above the High Altar. The large earthenware jar with a sealed lid contained a letter, handwritten on vellum, photographs of the church and a history of Woodford in 1860. The Reverend Christopher Smythe placed the jar in the roof of the church, in the hope that it would be found at some future date. The capsule was opened with great ceremony on live television, and has since caused a great deal of interest in the community.

It is not the first time that Woodford Church has been in the national news. In the 1960s, a photograph with the outline of a ghost, taken in the interior, not only caused a minor sensation on British television, but was flashed across the television network in the USA. Two boys, Gordon Carroll aged 16, and his friend David Hasdell, from Northampton, cycled out to the Nene Valley in 1964 to take photographs of churches in the area. On that particular July afternoon they chose Woodford Church and proceeded to take colour transparencies. There was no one but the two youths about at that hour. The slide that caused such controversy over the years was taken by Gordon at 2pm, looking towards the altar. When the slides were developed a few weeks later Gordon examined them but failed to notice anything unusual, and consequently filed them away in his large collection. A year and a half later he showed the transparencies at a family gathering at Christmas, and was astonished to see a kneeling figure in white on the steps of the altar. Each of the boys denied that it was a trick photograph, and even as adults have always stuck to their story that the ghostly image was as much of a surprise to them as to everyone else. Experts who examined the picture could find no evidence that it had been tampered with, and certainly the figure appears to be too detailed to have been just an error in the development stage.

Some are of the opinion that the shadowy ghost was that of a much-loved vicar of Woodford, The Reverend Basil Eversley Owen, who served from 1933-1955 and died in June 1963. Apparently, he would very often kneel in the very same spot as noted on the film. Another theory was advanced that it could have been the cleaning lady, taken as she swept the steps of the altar, but the two boys would surely have noticed her presence, even in the dim light.

A far more interesting suggestion put forward is that it is the apparition of Roger de Kirton, whose heart was returned for safekeeping. It may even have been the spirit of the knight who lies by his lady, immortalised in oak. Certainly, the figure seems to be wearing the long robe of the surcoat, as worn by medieval knights over their chain mail. Whatever the explanation, elaborate hoax or one of the unexplained mysteries, the only two people who really know the truth have always proclaimed the enigma to be a genuine phenomenon.

Incidentally, in the PG Tips tea packets there was a series of cards called 'Unexplained Mysteries of the World'. The Woodford ghost story is listed as number 26!

## Mansion of the St John Family

The mansion of the St John family stood on a field called the Warren, overlooking the River Nene and not far from the church. All that is left of it is a few humps and bumps and bits of the boundary wall. Built in 1621, it was an imposing edifice with fine terrace gardens. The first person to live there was Sir Oliver St John, who married Barbara St Andrews De Gotham. St Andrew later became adopted as a Christian name in the family. Oliver died at the early age of 37 years in 1661. His spouse, Barbara, put up a plaque in the church. She died in 1685 and was buried in the same place as her husband.

Two of their children were expelled from Oundle School after being accused of every kind of vice. It was probably one of these sons who became the next Lord of the Manor. He was St Andrew St John, who married Jane and produced a large family.

The last Lady St John to live in the manor, after her husband died in debt in 1767, was Louisa, who stayed on with her young children. Louisa had a boundary wall built in line from the old school in Church Street, down to the River Nene. She had an arched door fashioned in the wall, which is still visible today, for her convenience in walking to the church. People have claimed that they have seen the ghost of Lady Louisa gliding through this doorway! Her son had the mansion demolished in mysterious circumstances in 1786, after he was said to have found something disgusting about the dwelling.

By the middle of the 17th century, this family owned much of Woodford. The woodland now known as The Shrubbery was once part of their estate. Prior to the Enclosure Act, the village stone pits were located within these confines.

# Walk 26: Marston Trussell to East Farndon

*Marston Trussell – East Farndon – Marston Trussell*

**Distance:** 6 miles

**Terrain:** Easy but with many stiles

**Starting Point:** Church of St Nicholas, Marston Trussell GR 693859

**Map:** OS Pathfinder 937 Mkt Harborough SP68/78

---

This is a pleasant, level amble amid undulating countryside. The neat village of Marston Trussell lies 3½ miles south-west of Market Harborough, off the A427 to Rugby, and close to the border with Leicestershire.

**1.** Beginning at the church of St Nicholas, go right through the churchyard to a finger-post to Clipston then over two stiles.

**2.** Head for a gap into the Marston Trussell road and turn right.

**3.** In 20 metres, turn into Rectory Lane, where the slender tower of St John the Baptist, with battlements and pinnacles, rises on the hill. Beyond the farm buildings, look for a "public footpath" marker. Carry straight on, keeping the hedge on your right. Cross the next four fields to Dick's Hill.

**4.** Halt before the lane to turn sharp left to join the Jurassic Way to East Farndon.

Go over the stile then turn right to an iron gate. The church of St Nicholas should now be visible. Turn right soon to pass East Farndon Grange on the left.

Over the double stile, head for the church as you climb the hill. Atop the steep incline, take a breather to enjoy the view of the valley below as it spreads towards the Naseby battlefields.

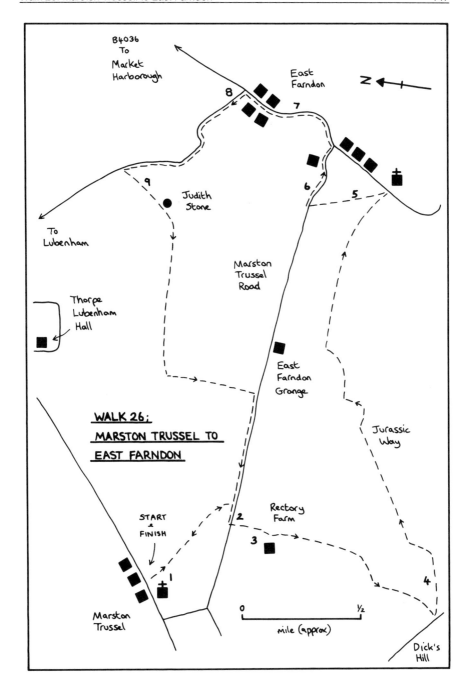

B4036
To
Market
Harborough

East
Farndon

**Z** ←|→

8

7

9

Judith
Stone

6

5

To
Lubenham

Marston
Trussel
Road

Thorpe
Lubenham
Hall

East
Farndon
Grange

**WALK 26;**

**MARSTON TRUSSEL TO**

**EAST FARNDON**

Jurassic
Way

START
&
FINISH

Rectory
Farm

2

3

Marston
Trussel

1

4

0                    ½

mile (approx)

Dick's
Hill

**5.** Still on the Jurassic Way, cross the earthworks below the church, then negotiate three more stiles and a gate giving access to the Marston Trussell road.

**6.** Go toward East Farndon, passing Hill Top Farm. In Back Lane note the date stone, inscribed 1664, on a house of brick and stone.

**7.** At the Market Harborough road, use the pavement for safety, passing Bell House as you approach the sprawl of the town ahead.

**8.** Cross to the 'village only' sign and the quiet Lubenham road. Ignore the first two finger-posts as you continue for half a mile. Lubenham Hall becomes more prominent as you progress.

**9.** Turn left on to the bridleway and proceed to the third iron gate, where there is a map and information regarding the Judith Stone, a glacial erratic (boulder) from the Ice Age, thought to be named after Countess Judith of Huntingdon, the landowner at the time of the Domesday survey.

Stay on the line, crossing over a track to the byway terminating at the Marston Trussell road. In less than a half mile, just before Rectory Farm Lane, return to the churchyard.

## Marston Trussell Church

Surely one can never tire of these ancient and enduring stone churches. They are often the comforting focal point of a truly rural English village, and nestle cosily among a mass of sheltering trees. The dark needles of the traditional yews are a reminder of defensive times in our history, when bows were fashioned from the slender, supple branches.

An interesting monument of a kneeling figure is in the church of St Nicholas. It is dedicated to Mark Brewster, who died in 1612. Simply described as a London merchant who perished 'in the city of Mosco in Russia', he was actually executed there. Described elsewhere as a 'pirate', this intriguing epitaph conjures up a mystery of some proportion, of an entrepreneur in a far-off land. But in what capacity did he earn this reputation?

Mark Brewster had retired to Marston Trussell in the hope of ending his days in peace and comfort, although Fate had other plans for him. He bequeathed to his church, forty pounds for a great bell, and also forty-one shillings and ten pence for the poor of the parish. An ambassador from Russia came to live in England and, by careful investigation, discovered the whereabouts of Brewster. The 'ex-pirate' was duly apprehended and sent back to Russia, where he was tried, condemned and put to death.

After the Battle of Naseby in 1645, bloody deeds were committed at the very gates of the church. The victorious Cromwellian soldiers hunted down the defeated Royalists who had fled from the scene of the battle to the confines of Marston Trussell. They gathered in a field close by, ever afterwards known as Slaughterford, where they made a last stand, although the struggle for survival was desperate and mostly hopeless. Some of the fugitives bolted to the church, where they hoped to gain sanctuary, but the parliamentarians cut them down at the portals.

These gates were badly damaged in the affray, when cannon balls (two of which were later dug up in the churchyard) were fired at the building. The Royalist soldiers who were killed in the skirmish were hastily buried together in a corner of the churchyard, now appropriately named Cavaliers' Grave.

## *Sunday Walks*

*As on a Sunday morning at his ease*
*He takes his rambles just as fancys please*
*Down narrow baulks that intersect the fields*
*Hid in profusions that its produce yields*
*Long twining peas in faintly misted greens*
*And winged lead multitudes of crowding beans*
*And flighty oatlands of a lighter hue*
*And speary barley bowing down with dew*
*And browning wheat ear on its taper stalk*
*With gentle breezes bending oer the baulk*
*Greeting the parting hand that brushes near*
*With patting welcomes of a plentious year*
*Or narrow lanes were cool and gloomy sweet*
*Hedges above head in an arbour meet*
*Meandering down and resting for a while*
*Upon a moss clad molehill or a stile*

This poem was written by John Clare, a Northamptonshire poet
who lived from 1793 to 1864. The county was quieter then,
but people still enjoyed walks in the countryside.

## Also about Northamptonshire:

### NORTHAMPTONSHIRE WALKS WITH CHILDREN

With this new guide by Judy Smith, families can enjoy discovering the secrets of Northamptonshire - an attractive but often overlooked county for walking. The 20, short walks are each presented in the form of a treasure hunt and observation game with questions to be answered and points to be scored on the history, fine scenery and excellent walking to be found in the area. Each walk starts from a playing field or recreation area and has suggestions for refreshment stops to keep the whole family going! *£6.95*

## More 'Mysterious' Walks:

### WALKS IN MYSTERIOUS SOUTH LAKELAND

Old Nick, witches, wizards monsters, fairies, and grizzly monsters! Graham Dugdale intertwines intriguing tales of these dark beings with his 30 skilfully chosen gentle walks in south Cumbria. "This is a well-researched guide book, well written, with a welcome thread of humour." THE GREAT OUTDOORS. £6.95

### WALKS IN MYSTERIOUS NORTH LAKELAND

Also by Graham Dugdale, an unusual collection of 30 walks which provide a unique opportunity to visit places with a strange and mythical history. "Each Walk.. features remarkable hand-drawn maps and stylish, entertaining writing that is almost as good to

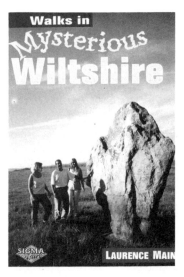

read before a roaring open fire as on the open fells" LAKELAND WALKER. 'Graham writes with robust enthusiasm...colourful excursions' KESWICK REMINDER £6.95

## WALKS IN MYSTERIOUS LANCASHIRE

Delving into a host of mysterious places throughout Lancashire, this unusual collection of 30 walks, suitable for all the family, will appeal to walkers with enquiring minds. From the enchanting follies of Lord Levenshulme of Bivington to the origins of the 'American Dream' in Worton, history and legend are inextricably linked in this succession of fine walks set in the superb Lancashire landscape. Lucid walking directions and the author's ornate, hand-drawn maps complement the entertaining commentary. £6.05

## WALKS IN MYSTERIOUS WILTSHIRE

Step into secret Wiltshire, one of the most mysterious of English counties, containing Stonehenge, Avebury, several white horses and now seasonally visited by crop circles! Laurence Main's 27 routes, suitable for all ages and abilities, take you into enchanting walking countryside, and a world of discovery. £6.95

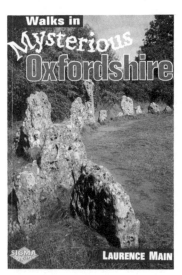

## WALKS IN MYSTERIOUS OXFORDSHIRE

Follow the leylines that connect holy hills and sacred sites, search for a lost giant, explore the river dedicated the goddess Isis and follow the spirit path to Banbury Cross, where the white horse overlooks Uffington. "...an attractively presented book which makes you want to pull your boots on and start exploring" BOOTPRINT. £6.95

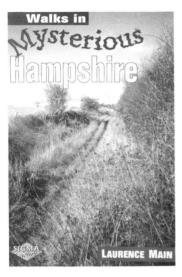
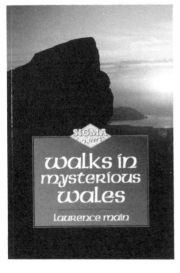